BELIEF IS THE NEW BLACK

BELIEF
Is The New
BLACK

Unlock Your True Potential by Discovering
The Power of Your Belief

MARNIE KAY
FOREWORD BY GINA MOLLICONE-LONG

Paperback - ISBN 978-1-77210-012-9

Ebook - 978-1-77210-013-6

Printed in the U.S.A

Chofesh Books, December 2014

Cover Design & Layout by Lauren Alicia

PROCEEDS FROM THE SALE OF THIS
BOOK WILL SUPPORT PLAN'S
BECAUSE I AM A GIRL INITIATIVE.
FIND OUT MORE ABOUT THE
INITIATIVE AT
BECAUSEIAMAGIRL.CA

Dedication

To my beautiful sister, Carls: you are my rock and my inspiration, which is no small feat.

To my best friend, my brother, Rob: even though this book is for girls you did wear my nightie once, and that counts.

To my darling niece, Hazel: may you only ever know how powerful you are, and nothing less.

To my dad, "You da best of da best of da best, SIR! with honors!"

Contents

Part Three:

GET A LIFE! (THE ONE YOU ACTUALLY WANT)

Foreword

I COULD TELL THAT MARNIE KAY WAS A FORCE TO be reckoned with when I first met her in early 2013. It was clear to me that she was willing to do whatever it took to get what she wanted. These types of people are my dream clients. They have greatness bursting at the seams, and they will leave no stone unturned when they are moving to the next level. All I do is show them how to get there faster and with less effort.

If there is one thing I've learned—one thing that I teach relentlessly—it is this: When someone doesn't want to change then there is nothing you can do to change them. And, when someone wants to change then there is nothing you can do to stop them. All of my students, my clients, and my audiences hear me speak those words of wisdom over and over again. Why? Well, it's exactly as Marnie says it is: belief is everything and everything is belief.

Your entire experience springs from the beliefs that you hold at the deepest level of your unconscious mind. I'm not talking about what you say to your friends when you want to look cool. I'm not talking about what you want to believe. I'm not talking about what you should believe. I'm talking about what you really and truly believe in the deepest core of your being. Your reality is a reflection of your beliefs. Period.

The surefire way to identify exactly what those beliefs are is to take honest stock of your life. Get real with how it is—not how you want it to be, not how you don't want it to be. Get real with how it is right here, right now. Then, just trace that outcome back to the only possible beliefs that could have created such a reality in exactly that way. Then, you will be face to face with exactly what you believe, even if you don't want to admit that you could possibly believe that.

The next step is easy. Just answer one simple question: how's that working for you? The step after that is even easier. You get to make a choice: either choose to keep empowering this belief or decide to let it go. Either way, it's your choice. No one can make that choice for you.

Fascinating research coming from the [1]Emory University School of Medicine is now confirming what we have long suspected in this field. Namely, that it may be possible for memories to be passed on to future generations genealogically. In their study, they showed that mice could pass on learned information about stressful and traumatic

2   1 http://www.nature.com/neuro/journal/v17/n1/full/nn.3594.html

events. Simply put, the mice could pass their fears down to future generations. Granted, further work needs to be done to confirm that the same chemical changes occur in the DNA of humans but, nevertheless, the finding is groundbreaking. Consider that some of the beliefs that you hold at the unconscious level, the very beliefs that may well hold you back from getting what you want, could possibly have come from experiences that weren't even your own. These beliefs could have come from previous generations. Now, how's that working for you?

Most people struggle with the notion that they are responsible for their life experiences. We have been duped into believing that the cause is someone or something outside of our own mind. True, you can never control the people or circumstances that surround you, but you can always control how you choose to see the world. This choice dictates your experience and your quality of life.

Perception is Projection. This is the main foundation of all of my Greatness U teachings, my books, my speeches, and my coaching with some of the most successful people in the world. Marnie is one of those people. She came with a powerful desire to change and an equally powerful willingness to do whatever was necessary to make that change —including, and most especially—giving up all the disempowering beliefs that had had a grip on her. I watched it happen with my own eyes. Desire and willingness are the two most potent qualities required when you want to change anything in your life, especially when you want to change your beliefs.

You will need the desire to get through the challenges of learning a new way of being. You will need the desire to get up when you fall down. You will need the desire to keep going. You will need the willingness to change when someone shows you a better way. You will need the willingness to persevere when your ego resists. You will need the willingness to let go when you have to give up a long-held belief. You will need the willingness to forge a new path when the path upon which you are traveling isn't where you thought it was going to be. This is called flexibility of behavior and it is the mark of true leadership.

I now repeat Marnie's wise words: belief is everything and everything is belief. Your life can be anything you want it to be, anything you believe it can be. If you could choose from an infinite range of possibilities then why wouldn't you choose the life that lights you up? It's all within your reach. It all depends on what you are willing to believe and what you are willing to give up believing. The key is in understanding that you are in charge of your beliefs and, therefore, you are in charge of your life. Greatness lies within each and every one of us. You only need to be brave enough to let it shine through you.

WRITTEN BY:
GINA MOLLICONE-LONG
Creator of Greatness U, International speaker, A Player Success Coach and best-selling author of "Think or Sink" and "The Secret of Successful Failing"

www.GreatnessGroup.com | www.GinaMollicone.com

Part One:
HOLD THE iPHONE! WE HAVE A PROBLEM...

Preface

AND IT'S NOT WHAT SHADE OF LIPSTICK TO WEAR or whether or not to eat the cupcake, although I too struggle with both decisions on occasion.

If you've ever found yourself crying for no apparent reason, unable to raise yourself from the horizontal position for daily livelihood activities or religiously sabotaging relationships like they grow on trees... this book is for you. I'm talking to you. In all your lipstick-wearing, cupcake-eating glory, even you know these are merely convenient replacements for self-worth, confidence, and self-love. Cupcakes can't love you back, sweetheart—not even the organic ones.

The problem, I believe is that we are simply unaware. We are unaware of our potential, our power, and of our connection to one another and the world.

The problem is whether or not we choose to love ourselves,

become who we are meant to be, and decide to light up the world with it. The world needs you.

In the midst of finishing this book I was procrastinating and resting on my perfectionist laurels quite happily until a dear friend reminded me (via a timely text message) of the very mission I was on... "Hurry up! The world needs you!"

She was right. I had something to give and I was holding it back. But I'm not the only one the world needs. Like most of us, somewhere along the way I forgot what I knew as a short creative blonde child. What I knew then was that anything was possible. I believed I could be a famous Hollywood actress by day and a doctor on the weekends all while I waited patiently for my knight in shining armor to come rescue me.

I knew that [2]The Splitz Club I had formed with my best friend in Grade 3 was to become an international success with girls all over the world wanting to join.

I knew that as an adult I would live in America for its summer season and Australia for its summer season (which was most of the year) so I could avoid winter at all costs. Who wants to live in the 'cold, dark winter' if they don't have to?

I knew I didn't have to.

I knew that a magical fairy left money under my pillow in exchange for my gross baby teeth, an obvious win for me

2 The Splitz Club was an all-girls club (membership appointed by me) that we formed to have girls practicing a specific gymnastic maneuver: the girls would spread their legs to opposite ends (either sideways or one out front and one to the back), and then lower themselves to the ground in a stretch. This was done ultimately to touch their 'hmm hmm' to the ground. This would take many practices for which we charged a small membership fee. The membership fee was used to supply candy for the club (courtesy of Marnie Enterprises).

(Marnie =1, magical fairy =0).

I knew that a simple kiss would heal all battle wounds, that the people we love will always be here, and I could be, do, or have anything I wanted.

I knew that my options in life were limitless and all I had to do was pick what I wanted. And it was boring to think otherwise.

The only limitation we have as children is our own imagination. Almost anything is possible if we can imagine it. Yet our imagination is the very thing we often leave behind with our childhood. That and The Splitz Club.

Let's be honest, The Splitz Club wasn't going to go very far. We kicked out more girls than we let in. But what about the big ideas that led to it? The imagination, the creativity, the empowering beliefs we had about our potential? We seem to throw the baby out with the bathwater, leaving it all behind in a hurried effort to grow up and be realistic—so we don't dream too big and fail, possibly? All the visions of possibility and reckless abandon that we so valiantly indulged in as children become distant fairy tales, eclipsed by what we think we should be thinking and doing as adults. Though I could state this more clearly by saying what our parents, friends, society, religion, culture, or social media outlets think we should be thinking and doing as adults.

Why do we so often abandon our childhood dreams and our wondrous beliefs about our future and what we are capable of?

The very few who don't abandon their dreams and beliefs go down in history as those who changed the world. The rest of us just stare in wonder and awe, as if that aspect of being human were never part of our own individual identities.

The reason we tend to get caught up in this abandonment of childhood dreams and beliefs is that we start to think about what we think about. We become afraid of the negative repercussions that failing or mistakes almost always bring. Teachers scold, parents punish, and friends taunt.

What was once encouraged, even considered cute when we were infants, failure, quickly becomes unthinkable, abhorred, there almost isnt anything worse, except, perhaps... hair static or chipped nail polish. We shudder at the sheer thought and, for all intents and purposes, forget it ever happened, we block it out.

This idea or belief that failure is bad leads us to begin to question ourselves. We second-guess what we are thinking in efforts to avoid further failure and consult those around us who are just as confused as we are (maybe even more so).

Then we either beautifully blossom or crash tragically into early adulthood and pretty much carry on in whatever fashion we arrived.

Don't eat the cupcake, don't dream too big, and don't fail.

Don't, don't, don't: it's all we come to know.

I crashed tragically into adulthood. Not much made sense

and I had no idea of what I wanted to be when I grew up. Everything seemed so far from possible that I felt stuck where I was. I had developed anxiety based on a fear I held that life was getting in the way of getting a life. I was stuck on a stationery exercise bike with no way off. And all I wanted was a cupcake. A red velvet cupcake.

While I probably looked like an outgoing, driven twenty-something woman, inside I was screaming for help, waving a big white flag in desperation just hoping someone would notice. I wasn't happy and, even worse, I didn't know why.

What I want you to know is that you are not alone, if I can get through my twenties alive you can too.

I don't know everything. I am not a scientist, doctor, therapist or psychologist. The only certificates on my wall are photos of the people I love. The only degrees I have received were in the 'thirds' usually by authority figures who think they know best (though perhaps they do). I don't come to you with endless knowledge from years of university. I come to you with experiences that have made me who I am. It is my intention to inspire you with imperfection in hopes that you find your own story along the way.

In saying this, I have devoted the better part of the last few years to going on an exploration, an adventure of discovery around the nature of belief. I have become fascinated with what belief is, where it comes from, and why it plays such a huge part in our lives. And, more importantly, I have become fascinated by what we can do about it.

There are many theories about our beliefs but most point to a general agreement on a few things that I want to summarize for you before we move forward. So I ask you to put aside what you know for a minute (remember, if you are like me, you once knew a magical fairy paid you for your teeth) and open your mind to the possibilities of a new perspective.

Here is what I promise to explore with you in the following pages....

1. Belief is an idea. A big one. What you do with it will determine your life.

2. Beliefs are often not our own but, rather, hand-me-downs. So watch whose old, smelly hand-me-downs you are wearing.

3. Beliefs are either empowering or imprisoning. They are the key or the killer. The beauty is you get to choose.

It's all you baby! You are more powerful than you think.

The question I have come to think about is why don't we believe that we are wonderfully creative beings that can live how we want, be who want, and feel a sense of happiness all the time?

Why do we hang onto beliefs that imprison us, limit our options and choices, before we even try? Why do we choose stories that keep us playing small instead of the grand lead role we were meant to play in our lives? Why do we accept a way of thinking that offers anything less than all the potential in the world?

I can't answer these questions for everyone. But in this book I explore the reasons I think our beliefs play a role in most of our decision making. Ultimately, I will share these thoughts so you don't have to make the same whopping mistakes that I have made.

Conveniently, most of the mistakes I have made can be traced back to one pretty big idea called out thousands of years ago.

"The problem is, we think we have time."
—Buddha

Unfortunately, only obvious in retrospect. Really think about this for a minute. We look at time as circular. It goes round and round. I own a circular watch (okay, I own a ridiculous number of watches) and a circular clock on my wall. The thing about a circle is that there is no end; therefore, thinking of time as circular and never-ending means our perception of time and our use of it is skewed.

There is always tomorrow or next week. There's always plenty of time to go after that dream next year, plenty of time to say I'm sorry, plenty of time to save or invest for retirement. I have lots of time—it just goes on forever like my watch.

But this is only a problem of perception. And a perception can be changed. It's all in how we look at it. Here is the first switch I'm going to have you make.

Don't think of time as clock, think of time as an hourglass.

It is running out. You don't know how fast that sand is making its way to the bottom chamber, so it's time to move. It's time to go after what you want and just do it.

Right? No?

Why not?

Oh, you're not good enough? You don't have enough money? You don't know the right people? It's too hard? (Insert excuse/limiting decision here…)

I can call BS as well as you can. These are just made up stories, limiting beliefs keeping you from your passions, your purpose, and what you really want.

Simply put: your beliefs rule your world.

But here's the [3]knicker kicker:

You rule your beliefs.

---

3 KNICKER KICKER — 'knickers' is Australian for underwear. Therefore, a 'knicker kicker' is a kick in the panties. You're welcome.

The stories we tell ourselves over and over again create and maintain the beliefs we hold on to, which in turn become the source of our feelings, decisions, actions, and reactions. Remember, these are beliefs that often aren't even ours in the first place. We all have beliefs about everything such as love, relationships, money, success, health, family etc. How much energy you give them will determine their impact.

Oprah Winfrey, one of the most successful women in the world today, has so eloquently said, "You become what you believe. You are where you are in your life based on everything you have believed."

So here we are, you and me. I have stories and you have stories, all of which carry some common beliefs that honestly we could do without, starting now. I share the following pages with you in hopes that you will join my journey, develop a new understanding of your beliefs and laugh with me along the way.

I once heard that a smart person learns from his or her own mistakes while a genius learns from other people's mistakes. As I've already made clear, I've made many mistakes and I happen to like sharing, so you get to be the genius. This is my gift to you.

Belief is
everything,
everything
is belief.

CHAPTER ONE
Belief is the New Black

1

The Introduction— Let's Get Naked!

I KNOW THIS IS ONLY OUR SECOND DATE, but I'm ready to get down to business.

When I said you are not alone, I meant it. Everyone's life and experiences are different, but the pain, the sadness, the confusion we can often feel is all very much the same. I am no different than you in many ways. By sharing our stories we can find a common thread of support and identification, as well as perspectives we didn't think were possible. Knowing you are not alone can sometimes be a significant shift in and of itself.

Let's take a little trip back to puberty: something we've all gone through to varying degrees. Close your eyes (after these directions) and think back. Remember a time where the effects of this hormone-inspired period (pun intended) of your life stands out, even today. Picture in your mind a memory, an experience, and float up above it.

Watch the memory or situation as it plays out. Use the following questions to help guide you into the vision of your former self:

What was happening?

Who was there?

How were you feeling?

What emotions were present during this experience?

Are there still there today? Or are they gone?

If you were in the same situation today, would you feel the same way? Or different?

Think of another example. Think of another time when you were compelled to feel a negative emotion based on the situation you were in. How would you react or behave now? Picture what was happening and who was there. Do you still harbor emotions toward those people or behaviors?

When you are done come back to the present time, and think objectively about what you saw. If you were to see someone else in the same situation, would your guidance instruct them to respond in the same way you did? If someone in the same situation felt the same way you did, would you encourage him or her to have a different perspective or meaning in order to help him or her move forward?

Having explored all of this, how has your perspective changed? How is your teenage self different from who you are today? What would you say to your teenage self if given the opportunity to interject on puberty and offer some much needed words of wisdom?

It's this objective position that will clearly spell out for you what was real and what was a byproduct of puberty. It will help you define what was worth your energy and what wasn't. Either way, all of it has shaped who you are, what you believe and how you respond in life today.

(Visualization allows for the imagination to create, recreate, and remember. This powerful exercise can become a beautiful foundation for change. Notice how you have a different perspective when you were outside yourself looking in? Visualization or meditation can give you the objective perspective that can help shape a more complete understanding of people, situations and emotion, allowing for a response more conducive to love, forgiveness and acceptance.) What a powerful practise!

Here are some of the things I remember from puberty. Aside from the horrifying Puberty Explained book my mum handed me (far too late, mind you, at age thirteen), there was no real introduction for what to expect from puberty. To be honest, I probably wouldn't have noticed beyond the cartoon birth pictures, but the book might have had more of an impact if it said something like this:

Welcome to adulthood, Marnie! I see you have a vagina.

Great news! Today we'll be serving an appetizer of debilitating anxiety with a side of unexpected outbursts and a main course of putting your dreams aside (you probably won't have time anyway). Our deserts this evening are a choice of feeling like you aren't good enough, an overactive imagination with an underactive metabolism, or our feature tonight... a bunch of limiting beliefs with a topping of some generalized comparison?

Probably an equally terrifying book to hand a thirteen-year-old. But it would have made a lot more sense; I was having more conversations about how I was feeling and less about my reproductive organs, which was likely my mother's biggest concern and the reason for the puberty book in the first place.

But all of these common feelings and emotions can leave us with an aftertaste of total confusion about our life and purpose here on Earth. I've consumed everything on this menu. And, as a result, I desperately tried to cling to anything that I thought I knew for sure. I needed to find something familiar, comforting, and safe. (Please just give me some certainty, something solid I can depend on so I can stabilize this s$#@ and catch a breath!) Enter... our beliefs, what we know for sure.

But our beliefs don't just show up unnannoucned to save

or ruin the day, they begin as an idea, an idea that grows. What we do with that idea determines how it impacts the rest of our lives. The idea can then become a fact or just one of those silly things we know isn't true anymore, like the magical tooth fairy.

Beliefs don't often start out as our own either. They are genetically and environmentally infused into our subconscious. They are most heavily influenced by the people and experiences in our lives and are usually the place from which we think, speak, and act.

Believe carefully, your life is as stake.

"For better or for worse, for richer or for poorer, in sickness and in health, till death do us part": beliefs are a part of us. What we believe is the reason we don't apply for a new job, the reason we always date the same type of person, and the reason we wear black to look and feel sexy.

My entire wardrobe consisted of nothing but black clothing. In fact, if you were to see me in a color, it was probably laundry day or forced upon me by a friend desperate to lighten me up. I had a certain belief about how black made me look and, as a result, it became the costume of choice. Whenever I would wear a black dress I felt confident, sexy, and life seemed effortless. I was ready to walk the red carpet—or rather, to the bar down the street.

Female beauty is often defined by the media today as tall and thin. Completely unrealistic for about 95 percent of us. This has drastically shifted since the era of the Marilyn Monroe 'hourglass figure', however, over the years black has maintained the ever-elusive intrigue of desire. The "little black dress" (LBD) was born out of the need to have a name for the garment we reach for when we most need to look and feel confident and sexy. As someone who has had a wardrobe comprised mostly of black garments, I am guilty as charged!

What I have come to learn throughout my twenties is that the feeling of being sexy or confident isn't necessarily the fact that the dress or top one chooses to wear is black itself; rather, it was the belief I had developed about how wearing black would make me look to other people—sexy and confident. I believed it made me look skinny and dark or alluring and, therefore, confident, sexy, and effortless. It really wasn't my own idea—meaning, I didn't come up with that on my own ; rather, it was because that's what modern fashion, culture, and the media suggest is beautiful and perspectively slimming for a woman to wear. In my mind, if it made everyone else more desirable, then it also made me more desirable.

So much power given to something so powerless. Imagine if we gave it to ourselves.

What classifies as beautiful in modern culture today seems to be more easily defined than ever before. Driven by mainstream media such as television, magazines, and movies (and now more destructively in our own pockets and purses via social media), we are absolutely told what to believe when it comes to feeling good about ourselves.

Have a look around. Take a look at your Facebook News Feed, if you have Facebook, or take a look at a few magazines, a television show, or even a few music videos on YouTube. How much of what you are seeing is suggesting something?

Find a few images you can focus on and pull them out in front of you right now. What do you see when you look at them? How do you feel? What thoughts pop into your head? What emotions come to the surface?

Pay attention to the internal conversation triggered by the image. What's the internal monologue sound like? Are there feelings of jealousy? Do you find you are comparing yourself or your life to the image in front of you? Write it down. Write down every thought as you look specifically at these examples. Fold the piece of paper and tuck it in the back of this book, because we will come back to this later.

So, if we equate wearing black with feeling desirable, then the idea or the belief that wearing black makes you sexy makes a lot of sense. But what doesn't make sense is the need to wear something in a particular style or color in order to feel confident, beautiful, and sexy.

What if we were to feel that way already?

Had I prior knowledge of this startling revelation, my wardrobe would have probably looked like a Skittles rainbow instead of looking like I worked the night shift at a funeral home. This is only one example of a belief that was inherited and subsequently indoctrinated. I'd be here all day reviewing the many others we subconsciously run around with, so perhaps I'll share that in another book.

As women today, what we wear is only relevant to the impact we can have in the world by how it makes us feel. For me, black was safe. And this is how I played for years, safe. It seemed the only obvious choice while I felt lost without a clear path or direction in life. At age twenty-six I quietly leaned on a walk-in general practitioner's diagnosis of depression and anxiety. Some days I believed I had depression and some days I didn't. I really had no other explanation for how I was feeling so I accepted this as the cause.

I didn't want to believe I had a choice. In no way did I feel strong enough to make a different one.

Wearing black constantly wasn't really a major concern for me (even if it was for my friends), I knew it was a symptom of something bigger. There was a reason I didn't feel good in anything else and strangely, it wasn't even the drastic fluctuation of my weight. I had found a dark place in my life. Actually, when I look back, it felt like it had found me.

It wasn't the first time I had found this darkness, but this time was different. I was barely able to sleep at night while I dragged myself through the days completely exhausted. It was all I could do to pull together enough energy to hide how I was really feeling in public—a total lack of energy or enthusiasm for anything. I felt worthless, like a failure, and I had found a new kind of desperation that was alien to me. I hadn't known desperation like this before. It was like my mind needed something to survive that my body didn't know how to get. I needed air but had forgotten how to breathe.

I lived this way, self-diagnosed with a case of 'lost and lonely' for a long time before I was urged to head to the doctor by a work colleague who was (unbeknownst me) watching me fade away. I just couldn't shake it. No amount of wearing black could magically bring me to life like it so often had before. While I didn't believe I needed the medication readily prescribed to me for depression and anxiety (a lethal combination of f'ed up), I realized I did need to admit I had a problem.

In order to move forward I had to accept where I was at in life. And that it wasn't where I wanted to be.

What's incredible to me is how little we understand about mental health. We know it's a feeling, a state of being or state of mind and we know some symptoms. No wonder it is estimated by the World Health Organization that half of the people in the world with mental health illnesses are undiagnosed. Canada, for example, is seen as one of the world's most affluent countries—with education and health care for the taking.

However, according to the [4]Canadian Mental Health Association, an average of one in four women will seek help for depression in their lives. This is estimated to be only half of all those suffering with it at some point. Even more staggering is that in 2013, 24 percent of all deaths in Canada between ages fifteen and twenty-four were suicide. I can only speculate what could possibly contribute to suicide at that age but having lived through that age range, I'd be lying if I said suicide hadn't crossed my mind.

This is obviously far beyond the concern of wearing black to feel sexy, but I can't help but wonder: Does it come from the same place? And, more importantly, what could change all of this?

Now that I am in my thirties (and on other side of feeling completely powerless), I now know how powerful we are. I believe we can change all of this. We are on the forefront of something

---

4 The Canadian Mental Health Association, "Fast Facts about Mental Illness." Retrieved from http://www.cmha.ca/media/fast-facts-about-mental-illness/#.VF_ pi4cbmcE.

huge—a revolution of feminine energy on the brink of understanding who we are and why we are here. And I can tell you it's for more than making sandwiches and beds.

As I enter my thirties, I look back at my emotionally charged teen years feeling as if it were lifetimes ago. It seems blurry and surreal, as if it were someone else's experiences and I had just borrowed the memories to serve a purpose in my growth.

What used to be thoughts of lack, can't, have not and 'I wish,' are now thoughts of yes, can, have, and 'I do.' It's as if suddenly I have new possibilities; I can see past the worries and the problems, and I just know everything will be okay. This is the hope I was searching for when I was younger. I just didn't know it would come from the struggles and pains. I thought nothing good could ever come from so much hurt and confusion. And yet here it is in all its glory. Clarity.

Now, when something challenging pops up in life, I hear the classic Bob Marley song, "Three Little Birds" start to play in my head:

Don't worry, about a thing

'Cause every little thing's

gonna be all right

My fingers start snapping and I start swaying awkwardly to the beat in my head. I know you're hearing it now, too. That's it: sway, snap, and enjoy!

This is a simple example of how we can change our emotions,

what we are feeling. I just didn't want to when I was younger. I identified with the negative emotions and the pain. I chose to be angry and hurt by my situations. Now I choose to sing Bob Marley and move on. I can change how I feel. We all can. What a powerful realization!

I can also tell you we are here for a good time, not a long time.

With all the beautiful love we give as girls, women, mothers, sisters, grandmothers, and daughters, we are the most at risk with the very thing from which we radiate, our big beautiful hearts. Our heart, from which we give and feel so much, is also the very place from which most women lose their lives. As per the [5]American Heart Association in 2013 "heart disease is the number 1 killer of women."

Heart disease. Why the heart? Many studies suggest nutrition, fitness and genetics can account for the cause (this much research I have done) but the heart is the spiritual center from which we balance every aspect of our being. Our heart represents the love, care, and compassion that we are made up of. It's the same love that has started movements, saved lives, developed nations, and transformed individuals all over the world since the beginning of human time. Why is heart disease so prevalent, and in women particularly?

For this question, I don't have an answer—at least not a scientific one, since I am not the doctor I set out to be when I was five.

5. "Facts about Heart disease in women," American Heart Association. Retrieved from https://www.goredforwomen.org/home/about-heart-disease-in-women/facts-about-heart-disease/

But I do have questions, some of which I have offered up in the following pages. Either way, both mental health and heart disease in women are largely unexplored outside of current scientific theories and yet both are very serious, life-threatening concerns. We owe it to ourselves to understand them as best we can. I can't help but feel they are somehow linked to each other more than we can explain. Both have touched my life in a way that has forever changed who I am and what I decide to leave behind as my legacy.

I have been very fortunate to be surrounded by many strong, loving women who at certain times in my life have been the guiding light, the beacon of hope. I think I speak for all of us when I say, we all have, whether in our family or community, or a little further away in history or the media. Women have changed and will continue to change this world. We have truly come a long way—from the days of being on a beach wearing a knee-length pantsuit (forbidden to wear anything less) seventy years ago and barred from any act of voting on political matters or elections just forty years ago. Despite all the advances that women have accomplished we have some of our biggest barriers yet to overcome.

In order to overcome the barriers out there, we have to overcome the barriers in here (pointer finger to side of head) and in here (other hand rests on left boob/heart).

Deep down we know this. I know you know somewhere in there that our toughest battles are within because I knew it, too. So, if all of our problems and solutions begin with us, then why do we often feel powerless to do anything about it? Enter... our beliefs. (Surprise!)

While we can look at all the challenges we face, the people or stereotypes that can get in our way, the statistics show that we are still marginalized and paid unfairly. These are just the result of what we think of ourselves, our beliefs and, in fact, in many cases these beliefs have been blown out, disproven by women who believed the very opposite is true instead.. Being a woman is only a problem if you believe it's a problem. And for some women it's not a problem at all. In fact, it's an advantage.

Men don't need to make way for women. Women need to make way for women.

And women more urgently need to pave the way for girls to show them whatever they dream is possible. It all starts with what we believe.

"What you believe has more power than what you dream, wish or hope for, you become what you believe."

—Oprah Winfrey

So let's get naked and wear belief instead, starting now. Naked. I can almost feel the discomfort from here! I'll go ahead and assume it's not a large percentage of women who are comfortable with this idea. I can only speak for myself when I say the reason we are uncomfortable is because we believe we aren't beautiful or perfect or what someone else would consider attractive.

The words *naked and comfortable* haven't been used in the same sentence for me since I was a toddler, when I was proud of my unusually placed belly button (it is higher than what seems to be average for everyone else). I simply wasn't comfortable with my naked self for a very long time. I had spent years building proof around a belief that my body wasn't sexy. I had worked hard on that belief.

I know I'm not the only girl who has ever had body issues, and this is why I am suggesting we metaphorically get naked now. Get uncomfortable. Get transparent. Get honest. We have to.

The only way to see the truth is to strip ourselves bare of anything covering it up. The truth is in there — under all the lies, stories, and limiting beliefs. We just have to find enough courage to undress, get naked, and come face to face with ourselves.

Allowing total transparency is one of the best gifts you can give yourself. It is acceptance and forgiveness and truth all wrapped in one.

CHAPTER TWO
Belief is the New Black

2

From the Land Down Under

No MATTER WHERE WE COME FROM, there is a likelihood that we share some similar beliefs. We also probably have some very different beliefs based on the culture, religion, and the social norms of our origin or environment.

Let me level the playing field and start by giving you a little background on the environment I grew up in. I promise to keep it short and hopefully amusing. I was raised in a small town in Australia in a typical average income family of five: two working parents and three rambunctious kids. We lived simply with the necessities and the occasional treats if we behaved while grocery shopping, but we weren't vacationing on cruises and sporting the latest gear to school when I was growing up. We lived in a beautiful house with a pool on the top of a hill in the 'bush' of a new development. My parents proudly built and landscaped my childhood home holding many memories of adventures, skinned knees, populating rabbits, populating guinea pigs, and a small caramel-colored pony named Fluffy. We didn't want for too much until we started going to school. That's when we started comparing our lives with those of our friends. It was only then that we noticed we weren't of the 'rich' variety of families. For the most part, however, we were very happy kids.

I was the eldest of two siblings, my sister Carly and my brother Rob. I was the self-proclaimed human guinea pig, the trial run of parenthood. My dad has often said he and my mum were strict during my upbringing because if they could get this child—raising thing right with me (the guinea pig), then the rest of my siblings would follow suit. I'm not sure any of this worked out the way they had imagined, but the last thing Carly and Rob did was "follow suit." So I played it as a sympathy strategy in the hopes my parents would loosen the rope a little on their parental control. Unfortunately, the rope remained tight.

My dad worked long hours managing a local government office in town, often coming home with horror stories starring screaming mothers, pregnant with four dirty kids running amok in the office, threatening to call the prime minister should she not get her hard-earned unemployment check. I actually think he enjoyed the challenges that came with his job. But he was tired, stressed, and missing something in his relationship with my mum. I could tell mostly by their limited interactions with each other but also the way he looked at her. It was as if he were confused.

He was and still is the silly dad, with the radical stories of his younger, freer days and idealistic views of the world (all of which I have gladly inherited). He did his best with a wayward wife who did as she pleased (also a quality I inherited). He took us camping to get out of the house, to the park to run around like maniacs and, on occasion, to the movies with a bag full of junk food from the grocery store on the way. With three kids, a trip to the movies was expensive enough, so he worked around some of the rules to cut costs.

We still did most things families did, just a little more awkwardly. For example, if we ever went anywhere requiring the purchase of an entry ticket (and there was a kids' ticket price option, usually for half the regular price) then we were all magically under age seven. This worked out well until I was about twelve, when I had had enough of being a child and decided against my dad's ushering me to "shut up." I began to proclaim my real age on the way in, valiantly.

A big hippie at heart, my dad was and still is a lover of all people, nature, and odd things. I lost count of the weird stuff he had collected that mounted our walls or guarded the entrance to doorways. He had collected stuffed birds, a goat head, an old turtle shell, a creepy old wheelchair from the 1800s, dead poisonous snakes in glass jars, homemade cement human limbs that stuck out of the garden to look like we had buried people, some nasty garden gnomes, and a partridge in a pear tree. He was truly a fine purveyor of weird shit. Thankfully, this is a quirk I did not inherit.

But I love him very much, and I've learned a lot from him about how to communicate my way out of things and into things, how to laugh off pain—physical or emotional and how to see things from another perspective. My dad is a man of love, courage, and a weird (though some would say sick) sense of humor. And, as much as my dad was confused by mum, he loved her.

They met while they were both very young when they were traveling away from home. My mum was the carefree spirit of the wild, and my dad was the funny, confident, loving man she was looking for. I don't know much of their early days, only that I arrived into the world by my mother's cunning plan and my dad's sweet ignorance. I was delivered to the world on May 26, 1984. They drove me home in a cardboard box.

My mum, soon after I was born, was diagnosed with severe postpartum depression. Not long after that, she was diagnosed with bipolar disorder and general manic depression. In the years she was with my dad she had singlehandedly mastered the appetizer, dinner, and desert menu I mentioned earlier. She was amazing and completely unpredictable. My dad just tried to keep up.

I don't remember much of my mother from a young age. I know she was often angry or upset. And she was known for sleeping in the bedroom with the door closed for days on end. She would also vacuum the floors for what seemed like days on end. I remember once when I was fairly little, probably seven or eight years old, and I was attempting to tell her a joke that I obviously thought was hilarious and needed to be heard by everyone in close proximity. She was vacuuming at the time, so I flagged her down, announcing I had a joke to tell. After a few 'not nows,' she gave in and angrily stepped on the pause button at the base of the sucking machine.

It was at this point I knew this joke had to be good, or else I'd have to apologize for interrupting a very important household task that required her utmost attention. So off I went with the elaborate knock-knock joke I had just heard on the television. I was nervous because I knew it would require more of her attention than she was willing to grant at that point in time (I could tell by the annoyed look on her face she had reached about a 2 out of 10 on the patience scale) but I went with it anyway.

Me: Knock, knock!

Mum: Who's there? (This was grunted between gritted teeth)
Me: Banana.
Mum: Banana who? (followed by another grunt)
Me: Knock, knock!

She lost it. "Enough!!" She announced she didn't have time to listen to a silly joke and stomped on the pause button so that she could resume vacuuming. I don't know what came over me at that point— normally I would walk away and sulk for a while, but for some reason I was determined to get to the punch line of the joke. The problem was I needed to get through four or five more bananas before I could even switch the answer to "knock, knock" with "orange"—"Orange who?" would be the answer, and then I would say, "Orange you glad I didn't say banana?" It was supposed to be long and annoying so the punch line worked.

I flagged her down again. "Mum, Mum! Pleeeeeaasseee, I wasn't done. Please just listen to the whole joke," I begged. I assumed she felt a little bad because she paused and stepped on the button at the base of the vacuum cleaner this time a little softer. It seemed like she had made the decision to try a little harder to be interested.

Me: Knock, knock!

Mum: Who's there?

Me: Banana.

Mum: Banana who?

Me: Knock, knock?

Mum: Who's there?

Me: Banana

Mum: Banana who?

Me: Knock, knock!

Mum: I haven't got all day. Can you just get to the punch line already? (Angry with gritted teeth again)

Me: But, Mum I have to do at least four 'bananas' before I get to the end! (Tears streaming down my face in frustration)

Surprisingly, she let me continue and, through the sobbing and sniffling, I started again to get through at least four 'bananas' in the joke before the punch line. I didn't get much further than the last attempt before she was vacuuming again, angrier than I even thought possible after a silly little banana joke. I never got to finish the joke.

That's pretty much how she was all the time. I don't have many memories of her being happy when I was a child. By the time I was thirteen or fourteen, however, I began to notice a change in her. Maybe she didn't feel we were as much of a burden on her life by then? Her depression was most extreme when we were young; as we got older it sort of faded away as if she were growing and learning to become the best mother she could be or instead, that it was easier for her to be our friend. It makes sense that we don't always start out knowing how to be the person we know we should be or even want to be. She just didn't know how to be any different, as much as we wanted her to be. Maybe the depression was how she coped with the gap? Perhaps what looked like not coping to everyone else was simply getting through the confusion for her?

This experience was one of many where I felt inadequate. I knew my mum was capable of giving her attention; I had seen it many times given to others and yet I had such trouble trying to capture it myself.

I thought I wasn't worth her attention. She didn't want me around. I annoyed her. She doesn't love me.

To anyone watching this situation play out, these conclusions would have seemed absurd; however, for me it was just more proof of the beliefs I was starting to build about our relationship and my worth.

You can probably recall a few times as a child where you may have had the same questions or a similar feeling because of something said to or around you. Simple suggestions, actions, words, or even the absence of such things in our childhood and adolescence become the foundation of our beliefs.

Every time my mum wouldn't listen to a joke, hid in her room for days, became angry at something that seemed insignificant, I just cemented another brick in the building of belief. My mum doesn't care about me; she only cares about herself. The truth was anything but. I was blinded by my belief. All I could see was what I believed.

I know she loved me in her own way. I also know I expected love from her to look different than it actually did. This was the beginning of our break down.

CHAPTER THREE

Belief is the New Black

3

You Are Not the Boss of Me

As I approached my early teen years I found a cool stubbornness that seemed to work well for me. I practiced often at home with a younger brother and sister who, by size alone, were destined to follow my instruction until they both grew bigger than me, like some sort of payback. I was large and in charge, unreasonably and painfully stubborn. It was a trait that at age fourteen actually landed me in more trouble than necessary. However, it was also a trait that as an adult is much celebrated and probably the reason I have achieved as much as I have.

Stay stubborn girls! Eventually stubbornness becomes strong-willed and independent, and this trait, can move mountains!

Early on in life, I decided that I was the boss and, boy, did that feel great. In primary school I was appointed school captain, a student leader who opens ceremonies, speaks on behalf of the student body, and represents the school at local events. I was appointed the role pretty much by a popularity vote. I remember overhearing one teacher suggest to another teacher that I should not have been given this position due to some minor class interruptions, a few lunchtime detentions and some general disobeying of the rules.

Like I said, I was the boss of my life. Part of taking ownership for who I was involved challenging the very rules that I was confined by. These weren't the big ones, just the ones that didn't make sense to me. By testing the rules set out by others I was able to determine which rules actually made sense to follow and which rules I could barrel through to lead a new path. As you can see I was full of some self-empowering beliefs; I simply hadn't learned anything different. Yet.

I finished my final year of primary school and my position as school captain to transition into the years of my life that would define me as a young adult, those high school years. The day I walked onto the school grounds of the new and prestigious Catholic high school (that had previously been an all-boys school until the year I matriculated there) was the day I found out I was already signed up for the student council. Again. I had just left a leadership position and its responsibilities behind so, being annoyed that I wasn't given the choice to take the position or not, I respectfully declined. The captain badge was cool, but I was allowed no real input on anything worthwhile. What was the point of that, I thought? I didn't need to be in the spotlight while I was busy trying to understand all the rules of the world by testing them.

Challenge the rules that don't make sense to you. Either for the purpose of understanding the rule set before you or for the purpose of going beyond it.

By declining the position I caused some political conflict; an agreement had been made between the local school board (which my dad had found himself a part of, also without much choice) and my previous school. Either way, I wasn't interested. My dad stood behind my decision even though I don't think he understood why. So I just went about my days easily collecting top marks with minimal input on the assignments at hand. This school needed to make a name for itself, and fast. The teachers were nice and generally forgiving, but the boss got even bossier.

Don't get me wrong here: I didn't boss anyone around. I wasn't the boss of others. By boss I simply mean that I was in charge of myself. I decided what I wanted to do and, for the most part, I did it. I spent some class periods in the girl's bathroom, where I recruited a fellow rebel friend to join me. We vacated the school grounds early, all without consequence, until one day they decided to crack down.

On that particular afternoon, a random assembly was called for immediate attention of the students and teachers out in the sports field. In Australia, during school hours, you have to wear a hat if you are not covered by some sort of shade. It's practically illegal to be in the sun without a hat if you are on school grounds. "Slip, slop, slap" was the campaign in the '90s that had everyone running for shade in fear of skin cancer. "Slip on a shirt, slop on some sunscreen, and slap on a hat." Rightly so, we knew of many people having irregular moles cut out of their skin at their local doctor (enough of a scare to take some precaution); however, very few were actually diagnosed with skin cancer. I guess this either meant we were doing a good job or we had gone overboard on the rules due to a kid who probably got burned in the sun at school. Either way, having no hat was equal to after school detention… was equal to death.

And so, on that afternoon, I hurried over to the crowd of students gathered by the entrance to the field, rushed by one of the teachers to get there on time to avoid a detention, and I was still issued an after school detention. I didn't have a hat on… damnit! They got me. How ironic was it that I was trying to run along so as to avoid getting detention and I get it anyway!

But I was determined to have the last word. I had bigger plans to get out of this school and start again. I was going to make new friends (not that there was anything wrong with the old ones), who would have no expectations of me.

Little did I know the rules that don't make sense don't stop at high school, or that high school in particular.

CHAPTER FOUR
Belief is the New Black

4

Life's a Beach

AT AGE FOURTEEN, a confusing time in my life, my mum had decided to enroll us in a sport that would give her an excuse (I think) to get away from Dad and be at the beach every Sunday: surf lifesaving. It was similar to the Ironman competitions or beach marathons for those who aren't familiar with the Aussie sport.

I immediately and completely fell in love with the sport. You couldn't get me out of the water or off the beach on any given Sunday. I was a naturally strong swimmer and carried an unnatural endurance for competition. I fell in love with conquering the wild surf, challenging teammates through the sand sprints and watching the older boys 'man' the beach, looking like Greek gods with their ripped abs. Apparently, this was also a bonus for my mum.

One 'beach man' in particular one to whom my mum had taken a liking, was the father of my two best friends at the time—they were twins my age. It was barely a few months after I had started attending the organized sport that one of the boys found me at the edge of the lifeguard tent and, while catching his breath after running from one side of the beach to the other, he made an announcement that he had seen my mother kissing a man while swimming in the surf. I knew exactly which man this boy was talking about, but I didn't want to believe it.

This was significant emotional event for me at such a young age. At the time I remember thinking, I'm fourteen now; I can handle this. So many new feelings and thoughts ran through my mind from that point on. It was like this opened the puberty floodgate of all possible emotions, and I quietly began to have conversations with myself to understand it all—to make everything make sense.

I couldn't talk to my mum about it. Or, rather, I didn't want to—which is probably more accurate. I was angry, upset, confused, and hurt. Each of those feelings would occur at different times for different reasons as I worked through all the meanings I could give it. Word spread fast that day and she knew I had found out. Her last words to me before we left the beach that day were, "You won't tell your father about this, will you." Her statement was not posed as a question but, rather, a statement. I was sworn in—so help me God. I wanted to run away.

But I didn't and, slowly, the whole story unraveled itself. My dad put the pieces together and, after some serious home life turbulence, Mum and Dad sat us down together as a family (which they had never done) to announce they were breaking up. You'd have had to be deaf and blind to not see that one coming, I thought, but my sister and brother were inconsolably upset. The arguments and fighting between my parents had just become a new level of normal for them. To them, it never meant they didn't love each other, just that they were angry at each other, all the time. The difference seemed blindingly obvious to me.

At this point, at least my mum had made a decision to make herself happy. This had seemed impossible until now.

Well, I'm sure you want to know the rest of the story. My mum went on to live with the man for whom she had developed an affection—the guy she kissed in the ocean, a man who eventually tried to kill himself on a number of occasions. He wasn't successful at any of the attempts but one time he came close. That time my dad was called in—thanks to a last minute distress call from my mother's best friend. She didn't know who else to call, she said. My dad, the hero, arrived at the scene begrudgingly until he realized the severity of the suicide attempt. He broke through the window of my mother's house with a brick and, after failing to find a pulse on Mum's new boyfriend, he called an ambulance just at the right time to save his life. Can you see the irony of that? He had saved the life of the man for whom my mother had left him just a few months prior. This is where my unwavering respect for my dad comes from. I do not know many people who could or would put everything aside to come to the rescue. My dad didn't leave his superhero cape behind with his childhood. He still wears it today.

My mother's decisions at this time in my life became questionable to me, along with this new guy's intentions. I couldn't separate what was happening around me from her ability to make better decisions. I started to believe it was her fault. So I decided to spend the majority of my home time with my dad at his house. This seemed like the more stable, less confusing option for me. Little did I know this decision would impact the family for many years to come.

CHAPTER FIVE
Belief is the New Black

5

The Great Divide

It was a year or so later that my mum and her boyfriend broke up. She decided it was over after he started hiding her jewelry and putting sugar in her gas tank to stop the car (and her I guess) from going anywhere. My opinion of her decision-making improved slightly at this point, but my expectation of her did not.

This is when I had started to become confused by her. I guess, like my dad, I was baffled by what seemed to make sense to her. I had distanced myself from her, almost in revolt, so as not to be associated with what didn't make sense to me. She seemed to be this enigma I couldn't figure out. The hardest part was seeing my dad hurt and alone. Left behind, confused and a little lost after fifteen years of trying to figure my mum out, he probably realized he never would. My sister and brother, so young and bewildered, decided to live with my mother. Here began the great divide.

My relationship with her became constrained, forced, and untrusting. She viewed my choice to live with my dad and visit with her less often as a definitive statement I was making about my preferences between the two of them. I began to resent her seemingly poor decisions, and the fact that my younger sister and brother had been exposed to it all. The gap grew bigger.

Mum went on to date other men, most of whom we three kids didn't like (I'm not sure she did either: she eventually found some nonsensical reason to push them away.) But I do know she was looking for something—more than what she had. She was searching for something bigger, something dream-like.

I know now because, as an adult, I was looking for it, too.

It took me until a few years ago to realize we were looking for the same thing, at different times in a different existence and yet somehow it's all connected.

Ever since then I had blamed her for everything. My mum Wendy became a convenient scapegoat for me. She is the mum, and she should know better, right? This is the story I would tell myself so much that it became the belief I hung onto until only a few years ago. It was a belief I had held, a grudge I had developed, that helped me make sense of all of it in my confused young mind.

That became a part of me as I grew up. It was something of which I could be certain and with which I could be familiar among the chaos of life. It gave me a reason to justify why I felt hurt, and it gave me a reason to give up on things or not try. It gave me all the reasons to sit back and let life happen to me.

What's so incredible is to look back on that story, that belief I had created. What's even more incredible is the fact that I had convinced myself that it was true, and it caused so much damage, not only to my relationships but to me. It was simply justification at it's best. Either way, I lost.

What if I had just told myself a different story?

CHAPTER SIX
Belief is the New Black

6

Me, Myself, and the Holy Grail

M<small>Y</small> TEENAGE JOURNEY FOUND SOME NEW challenges. I managed to harness all of this energy and channel it into a job answering the phones and placing orders at a booming Chinese restaurant in my town. I was fifteen at the time. I found something I was good at other than blaming. After a year of learning the ropes, my inner boss was put to work leading the serving staff of the restaurant and front desk take away. It seemed a bit ridiculous to my family and friends but I was quite comfortable being the boss. This time, however, I was being paid and it was a position to which someone had appointed me. I took on the position wholeheartedly, training the new girls that had started and hustling the older ones to move faster. It was bad enough they never cared as much as I did to get the orders right and the meals delivered to customers on time. It was even worse to expect "service with a smile" in the process.

This is one of the simplest things I've learned about dealing with people. It doesn't take much to stand out—just care more and pay attention. You'll look like a rose in a bed of weeds. And, smile, for goodness sakes! People like it when you smile!

Someone once told me that everyone is wearing an invisible sign around their neck that says 'love me.' This makes sense to me because I'm wearing one, too.

I worked this way everywhere I went. Later, when I was seventeen, I managed a gas station for a young guy who owned two of them in town. He never seemed to be around much or too available and suggested once that his new girlfriend was the one taking up all of his time. I was signing off on gas purchases from truck delivery companies in my miniskirt with green eye shadow and a flower clip in my hair. The owner would waft in every few days and clear the cash into his pockets, eat a candy bar off the shelf, and fill my car up with gas for free before he left.

I didn't care as long as I was paid on time, which was the case most of the time. I actually liked the freedom, although I often wondered why he left me there alone. He really had no clue what was happening in his gas station at any point in time. There could have been monkeys handling the gas pumps and my childhood pony, named Fluffy, at the cash register for all he knew. I figured it out, though: he trusted me. He knew that I cared, probably more than I should have.

As I finished school and went on to university, I resigned from the gas station, much to the disappointment of the owner (he said he couldn't trust anyone else). He would have to figure it out because I was moving on to university, which was a big deal in my family. Not a lot of people from my high school went on to university. Almost a third had dropped out of school at the completion of grade 10 to take up a trade, which was a booming industry at the time. And of the rest, some went on to the next level of education, but most went on in search of something other than school. Maybe twelve years had been enough already.

My chosen course of study was theatre. I loved the stage. The thrill of playing an exaggeration of someone other than myself, the pressure of remembering lines, and portraying an emotion I probably hadn't felt yet drew me in. Shakespeare, sixteenth-century commedia dell'arte, the Greek history, the passion: I loved it all! I had been accepted to a few universities both for a degree in either theatre or journalism. Both were my passions at the time, both were creative, dramatic, and exciting to me. When it came time to make a decision, clearly I chose the more fun option. I didn't put much thought into life beyond university, but why not do something that I loved? The rest of my life I would just have to figure out later.

I am so very fortunate that my family seemed to support my decisions in life—at least they didn't stand in the way. It was an accomplishment in my family to go to university since most of my family hadn't. I could have said I was going to get a degree in shoes and they would have probably thrown a party. So off to university I went.

CHAPTER SEVEN
Belief is the New Black

7

Real Life Gets Real

E<small>VEN AFTER THE BUILDUP AND ALL THE HYPE OF</small> UNIVERSITY ITSELF, my experience as a university student was short lived. It lasted a year. Rather, I should say, I lasted a year—I'm sure it carried on well enough for those who didn't quit.

The decision I had made to leave university wasn't a big one for me. I had gone into debt to attend in the first place, so I wasn't on the hook with my parents for the bill. I had chosen theatre over journalism, at the time a choice of passion and fun. It was something I really wanted to become good at. I really wanted to be an actor. My first and only year in university was everything I thought it would be: I was learning a craft and developing great friendships, but I had come to a big realization that I probably didn't need to go to university to do this.

I started learning about the industry and that there were many other theatre and acting schools that more intensely focused on the craft and the opportunities. I auditioned for a theatre production and garnered one of the lead roles of an eight-week show with no preparation. So I knew I didn't need the degree to live the dream as I had once believed. So what was I still doing there? I had just fallen into the habit of continuation with no real thought as to what I was doing and why I was doing it, other than the fact I was having fun. Somewhere in there I had rekindled the fire of my ambition. Remember the rebellions of my younger years?

Maybe I had become bored with just 'having fun', but it no longer served me to do just that. I wanted more. So I turned to my part time work at the music store. My ambition had a place here; there were opportunities on the table for me to apply myself and manage, make more money, and lead. So I took them. I was offered a management position at a store over the Christmas holiday period to see if it was for me before I was to begin my second year of university. I decided to make the most of it.

Once I was making a full-time salary income and in the groove of managing my own store, the thought of a second year fumbling around in a theatre degree with no real direction or career seemed unattractive. I was on a path, a clear one with goals and opportunities and I was good at it. So I stuck with it. Two years later I was promoted to the role of area manager, overseeing twelve locations. This decision paved the way for my entire career, my entire life. Once I was in the habit of getting results, leading people and making money, there seemed to be no other option. I had no degree, no other school to fall back on. This was it.

I happened to like earning money. It wasn't the cash in my bank account; I would spend it as fast as I made it. It was the feeling of freedom, that I could go anywhere and do anything or have anything I wanted. There wasn't a restriction on what I could pay for to do fun things.

Money = fun

I grew up in a town that was known for its high incidence of crime, teen pregnancy, and poverty. It wasn't uncommon for teenagers to drop out of school at the completion of Grade 10 and begin a career in a trade such as woodworking, metallurgy, construction, or mining. My dad managed the local government office for many years; he saw the worst of the worst. There were starving families and homeless individuals, as well as the complications that come from drug and alcohol dependencies or addictions. He was often threatened by some of the patrons (sometimes violently with weapons), and they argued with him and harassed him. This office in particular had a reputation for having one of the highest volume of clients out of all the government offices in Australia. It was certainly one of the most difficult to manage.

I grew up with friends who became heavily involved in the drug scene. Some left school, some turned to lives of crime, and some ran away from home. It was a fine line for me to choose the path I did, and the choice was always to follow my father. I felt that I could just have easily gone the other way.

I had a belief that the decision was either-or. Either I followed my friends and lived with no real passion or purpose or I followed my father, who had a very solid work ethic and received a great deal of positive recognition from those around him. The choice seemed easy. I looked up to my father very much. Every time a decision came my way, I may have dabbled on occasion with something unsavory, but I would always come back to the path he was on.

As I developed more responsibility in different jobs, I felt proud of what I had accomplished. My dad was also proud of my accomplishments. Once I believed I could work my way to pride, admiration, and success, I couldn't get enough. That positive recognition became the driving force, propelling me to succeed in just about everything I was doing. Success became very much like a drug. If I failed or didn't exceed the expectations I set for myself, I would beat myself up to no end and make a decision to work even harder. The harder I worked, the better my results would be: that's what was constantly going through my mind.

My competitiveness came from the need to feel successful,

as well as the pride I had tasted at a young age. There was a direct correlation between what I had witnessed my dad receiving from others watching my dad always come out on top with the best results. I was out to prove to myself that I could be great, the best and anything less was not good enough. It was always my priority to be number one, no matter what it took—whether it was eighty-hour workweeks, no days off, or doing everything myself so as not to disturb others. I believed that my subordinates would like me more as a leader if I could do more for them. As you can probably imagine, that didn't turn out to work very well. It became an expectation: Marnie will do it. Marnie will help. Marnie will take care of it.

At a young age I started to understand that most things in life causing stress for my parents were related to money. And anything I wanted in life would cost money. Money, like success itself, became a central focus for me. Just as I had thought the harder I worked, the happier I would be, the same was true about money. The more money I had, the more things I could do. And, most importantly, I could avoid the pitfalls of money-related stress that seemed to plague my parents often. Money equals fun was the exchange I identified with—that and work equals money. You can see how working hard equals money was a natural progression in beliefs for me, and is for most people in the world.

So I channeled my inner boss, worked just a little bit harder than everyone around me—with a smile!—and was promoted multiple times until I become the area manager of the state of Queensland. I was overseeing twelve music retail stores at the age of nineteen. That was unheard of in the company and, I'd suggest, even the industry at that time.

I would often sit in boardroom meetings with my orange juice while everyone else had coffee. It became a running joke that I wasn't old enough to drink coffee. I would laugh cordially, join in their jests, and then go about my day getting the best results in the company. I was out to prove that age and gender wouldn't stop me. And, aside from working sixty hours a week and a few nervous breakdowns, I was the best. But what was the cost? I began seeing some of my strengths drive me to anxiety.

I was building mental and physical habits around a belief that I had to prove something to someone. Being the best meant that I was a better person somehow.

I remember when I was struggling in my early days as a new area manager. I was overseeing brand new managers in each store, insurmountable boxes of product to unpack and merchandise along with a few human resources concerns that I had absolutely no idea how to manage. When the company's results by area came out each week from head office, I was ranked second on a list of twelve area managers. Note that I was second and not first. I wanted to be in first place so badly, but this guy, Matthew, from Sydney stayed on top every week by the slightest percentage over me in sales. Here was Matthew, always first with his smug smile and his fantastic results. I didn't let many people I didn't really know consume my thoughts too often, but I laid awake at night thinking about this guy.

I finally asked my boss, the national manager, one day, "Why? Why does Matthew continue to exceed my results and be number one?" I felt like I was working harder than ever. My boss replied, with a bit of a giggle at how distraught I was, "Marnie, you are only ever as good as your weakest link. You are a great leader, but that doesn't mean your teams are as good as you. Matthew has developed amazing leaders, so it doesn't matter how good he is; they get the results for him." It was like the sun had risen above the clouds and my eyes were opened for the first time. I was doing it wrong. It wasn't about me.

In order to be great, I had to help other people become greater.

Well, shit! Here I was trying to improve my own efficiency in selling new releases, unpacking boxes, and hiring and training staff nonstop seven days a week. I had always been told, "Work hard and you'll get the reward. Work hard and you'll get the reward." I believed it, too. I had been driven by this belief in all my other jobs. But what had led me to results in an individual contributor environment, was not what was going to lead me to results in an environment that requires team effort. I expected the same results and the same praise but the harder I worked, the more work I got. The employees in the stores I was managing had developed a belief that "Marnie will do everything for us."

I remember that realization to this day; it changed the course of my entire life. Thank you, Matthew. We both win.

I made plenty of mistakes early in my career. And rightly so. I was arrogant and felt invincible; I used it as a playground to experiment. For me, it was similar to school. It was a place to test the limits of how far I could go. After all, I believed I was one of their strongest area managers and I believed they wouldn't fire me. My secret was that I was just making it all up as I went along. I am a great listener, watcher, and modeler. I can pinpoint success and what it looks like and then emulate it. Success leaves clues, right? Fortunately, this was the only grassroots company I had ever worked for that allowed a nineteen-year-old to hire and fire at will. Let's just say I narrowly avoided a few minor litigation situations, other than that I was very successful for a 19 year old girl.

What was the reason for my success at such a young age? I was a university dropout, I was in a heavy metal band for a little while, and then I was replaced (P.S., you need to be able to sing).I gave up on my theatre career (P.P.S., you still need to be able to sing). I felt all I had left with which to prove myself was my job. So prove myself I did. I made it a personal mission to work harder than everyone else around me, get better results than everyone else around me, and to never see myself as anything less than capable of the next promotion. It became my identity. Little did I know I was building a big fat house of cards. It was all a grand illusion.

I had built this house of cards for a long time. It had worked for me, fanned my ego. There was always someone to prove myself to, and the endless promotions, awards, and salary increases. By the time I was twenty-seven I had done it all. I had moved to Canada, exploring the world and the opportunities available in it. I had taken on a new position in human resources (surprising, considering my earlier misfires) overseeing eastern Canada and the United States for a major fashion brand. I had no formal training in human resources.

I oversaw multiple 100-million-dollar retail businesses with thousands of employees, hundreds of leaders, and usually a head office with an agenda more important than my vacation requests. It was a big shit sandwich of other people's needs, and I was in the middle.

I had gotten smarter, though. I was often faced with problems I had no experience handling, and I was being paid a six-figure income plus bonuses to drive strategies, sales, and mitigate loss in the process.

I realized along the way they weren't paying me because I had already faced every problem possible, these companies paid me because I was an expert at surrounding myself with the right people (remember Matthew?). I hired the best, made sure those around me had whatever I didn't and led the team—people first. That and I worked harder than anyone else. By all appearances it seemed as if I had it all. That was the illusion. In the office I was the driven, confident thought leader I needed to be to get the job done.

Outside the office, however, I was a complete mess, failed relationships, I was pretty well broke (no idea how on a six-figure salary) and alone in Canada with all my family back in Australia. I hadn't spoken to my mum in over nine months. I had ignored a birthday card she sent me with 100 dollars in it, and I also didn't send flowers to her work on Mother's Day as I had done every other year. I can't even remember to this day what the catalyst was to launch this nine-month-long relationship standoff with her. Gradually we just stopped communicating.

My weeknights and weekends consisted of drinking and spending money I didn't have on stuff I didn't need. I should have been happy with the success in my career, if nothing else, but there was something missing. I felt it deep inside me—deep in my soul. I needed something to change. I just didn't know what.

Looking back on the situations I found myself in while I

thought I was moving up the corporate ladder, I can clearly say that I was a bit of a Lone Ranger. You know the Lone Ranger from the early days of television? He would go around solving problems and then ride off into the sunset alone. Someone would ask at the end of each episode, "Who was that masked man?" to which another person would reply, "Oh, he's the Lone Ranger!"

In fact, most of the things he did were alone—well, there was his sidekick, Tonto, and his horse, Silver. And he wore a mask, for Pete's sake, so he was trying to cover his identity. In other words, he didn't want people knowing who he really was. He didn't want people to even give him credit for the things he was doing. Perhaps it was because he thought no one would be willing to step up to the plate and fight injustice in the same manner that possessed him. But, knowing what I know now, it must have been extremely exhausting.

I think there was some pride in accomplishing things by myself; I believed as a leader if I couldn't do it myself then I probably wasn't a very good leader. Lack of action on the part of my subordinates would ultimately reflect poorly on me. Bearing the burdens of responsibility was something I thought people in authority were supposed to do.

At one point of burnout, I remember my boss, the national manager of sales, had called me to ask for something when I was at the tipping point. I burst into tears on the phone (much to his surprise) and he asked me what the problem was. I let it all out, for the first time ever I couldn't hold it in anymore—all the stress of work overload, the anxiety of needing to get results became a total outpour of emotion. He asked me in the midst of all it, "Marnie, why didn't you call me? Why didn't you just ask for help?" I realized if he was laughing then it probably wasn't life or death.

Again, I didn't have an answer. I knew he was right. And I knew it was my pride—my need to do it myself, to be the best, most reliable person, and perfect... by myself. Well 'perfect' had exploded in my face. He laughed at me, sobbing through the phone without an answer that would make sense outside of my own head. I realized if he was laughing then it was probably wasn't life or death like I had built it all up to be. It was a big fat belief that my success was a matter of life or death. That governed every decision I made.

This need to do everything myself and claim the prize was sabotaging me. I couldn't do my best when I wasn't at my best so I would work more and push myself further. I had watched so many people I respected in my life do the same; why should I have an easier time of it? This was just how one became successful.

I had learned in school that effort, activity, and involvement counted. The teachers praised all three of these qualities. The same went for work. I made an effort to smile, connect, and entertain guests and customers. I would ask my boss what else I could do to help. I carried this over into my career—creativity, initiative, and culture exuded in my work ethic. I knew my presence was appreciated when I watched my peers and workmates scowl. They would complain and try to do the least amount of work.

The initiative I took was an easy stepping stone into leadership. Most leadership is initiative; the only other option is complacency, or to follow. I had the awareness of what could be done, the willingness to do more, and the attitude to do it with a smile. Either I naturally led people by way of influence or the initiative I took eventually included them anyway, whether they liked it or not. Nevertheless, I still wasn't happy or fulfilled.

The funny thing about life is, you get out of it what you put in it. It often won't change unless you do, or you need to.

CHAPTER EIGHT
Belief is the New Black

8

When the Hourglass Runs Out

I WAS OUT TO PROVE TO MYSELF THAT I COULD DO anything I set my mind to. Anything anyone else could do, I could do better. I could only be proud of myself, and my confidence survived on my results. I looked outside of myself for recognition and praise to validate my worth. And I often got it, but not without a lot of hard work. I exchanged my work ethic for confidence.

Everyone I considered successful—including my dad, my first area manager at the music stores, the national manager when I became an area manager of sales and many other leaders I looked up to over the years —worked more than necessary. They worked to the bone, to the point of exhaustion. In retrospect, my belief that work ethic meant success makes a lot of sense, when you look at the role models I looked up to.

They all had what I wanted, so I mimicked their activities

and mannerisms. It seemed to me to be a simple formula; I would get what they had if I did what they did.

But I knew I was at the end of the rope. I was hanging on but barely. I was submerged in a state of depression, with extreme bouts of sadness where I wouldn't leave my bed for days. I avoided most contact with the real world and had to reach deep for every ounce of energy I could find to keep the tears inside while I worked at a job I was beginning to resent. I would survive all of this each day just to come home and go through it all again the next day. That's not living. I think that's actually dying.

It was like I was waiting for something drastic to happen to pull me out of it. I was waiting for something outside of myself to change this miserable life I had created where the only sense of being alive I felt was an occasional evening or weekend with friends involving the consumption of a ridiculous amount of alcohol. This was it: work, drink, sleep, repeat.

I knew I couldn't carry on this way. I had lost the strongest version of myself long ago. I guess the world was tired of waiting for me to change, so this time life took change. That drastic change I was waiting for showed up in the worst possible way.

The hot July weekend of 2011 was the break from work I needed. I was headed off on a road trip for music, booze, and more booze. My best friends at the time had purchased a ticket for me to get me out of the city to one of the country's biggest music festivals. I was actually excited. I loved everything about what this weekend promised me. We drove out at dawn, to Montreal, a city about seven hours away to settle in for three days of good times.

I had to negotiate amongst the other leaders for the weekend off from work, which was the final straw. I literally had to beg for the time off to take a small trip, which finally pushed me over the edge. I had reached a breaking point. I was determined finally to make a change when I came back. This weekend would be a great getaway, I decided, to clear my mind and come back refreshed. Then I would be ready to make some real decisions about how I wanted my life to be.

The weekend was everything I had expected. I partied, I drank, I danced, and I partied some more. It was the escape I had been looking for. As we wound down the party and left the scene where thousands had joined us for three long days, I began to dread heading back home to real life. I had to face some actual decisions if I really wanted change. And, ultimately, to be happy I knew it was important to make those changes.

I left the music festival on a complete beer/live music-induced high. As we slowly dawdled our way back to the hotel, I realized I had missed some phone calls on my cell phone. I really hadn't paid attention to it the whole weekend, which was refreshing. The missed calls I found were from my sister, Carly, which sent some irregular shivers up my spine. She never called me on my cell phone unless we arranged a time to talk. I almost didn't think anything of it until a gentle nudge from my friend urged me to call. "Just in case," she said. So I called my sister. The 'just in case' phone call sent my entire world—everything I thought I knew, the mundane life I had slumbered into—crashing down around me.

I remember the words my sister had said, the ground as I stumbled along trying to process the information, the warm breeze on my face and the pitiful city trees cemented into the sidewalk- like it was yesterday. It was only a few minutes but that one phone call felt like the entire length of my final year of high school, painstakingly eternal yet I didn't want to hang up. Through her sobbing on the other end of the line, all I could make out was the muffled repetition of my name.

Marnie. Marns!

'What?' I asked suddenly feeling a wave of terror come over me. 'What happened?' A million thoughts ran through my mind, she was seven months pregnant- what if something went wrong? Her husband worked in the mines underground- what if something happened to him? My beautiful, very pregnant sister was trying to tell me something and I knew it was bad- I could feel it. All that I could think of wasn't anything close to what she was about to tell me.

"Marns, it's Mum, she died. This morning. We don't know

why- Rob found her and I don't know what to do- I can't stop crying. It's aweful!"

I was speechless. My mouth was open but nothing was coming out. I think I managed to spit out the question "Are you sure?" followed by a few desperate pleas "Not yet! Not yet! I haven't fixed it yet!"

I was heartbroken, confused, and in shock.

Nothing can ever prepare you for this moment and yet it's something most of us are destined to experience at some point in our lives. I just didn't think it would happen to me.

I spent the next few hours in complete disbelief as I sat on the floor of the hotel room trying to find the next flight home on my laptop. All I could think was Why? Why her? Why now? Why me? My poor friends sat on the floor with me with no idea what to do or say.

Once we confirmed a flight, we began the long drive home to Toronto so I could take the first flight out the following morning, home to Australia via the longest route possible, as the booking was so last minute. I was dreading it all. I stumbled around the room just moving things from place to place instead of into the bag I brought it all in, until my quiet friends took over to hurry along the process. The worst forty-eight hours of my life was spent traveling to Australia with no idea of what to expect on the other end.

There was one thing I knew for sure. Mum wouldn't be there to pick me up from the airport. She wouldn't be there to say everything would be okay. I was going to have to find some strength to say, It's going to be okay in her place, for my pregnant sister and my little brother who had lost his best friend.

I had no idea where this strength would come from. I felt weak, helpless, lost, and scared.

The following weeks were a blur. My brother, my sister and her husband, and I all slept in the living room of my mum's house, piled onto the floor on a few mattresses we had pulled from the bedrooms. We couldn't be apart. We huddled together just trying to make sense of what had happened. We were mostly quiet, in thought (we must have cried alone trying not to upset each other), but there were some funny bits in all of it, exaggerated by the disbelief in the whole thing, I'm sure.

One thing in particular from that period I remember clearly. We had to design the funeral day, the last thing any of us wanted to do, and yet not one of us sat out of the conversation. It came time to choose the coffin. Never did I ever think I would have to pick a coffin for anyone. As we quietly flipped the pages of the coffin catalogue we were almost at the end of the booklet without having chosen any that we liked, until one of the final pages turned and we stopped to lean forward over the table all at once. It was a pearl white casket with gold handles and a gold nameplate. We all looked at each other as if to agree instantaneously on the same one and my sister blurts out, "It's perfect! I love it!"

What she had just said forced her to recoil with her hands covering her mouth, as if she couldn't believe what left her lips. She screamed out half laughing half crying, "I mean... I don't love it! Obviously, I don't love it!"

We all burst into a fit of laughter, tears streaming down our faces as we let go of some of the emotion we were hanging onto in a beautiful, hilarious moment that I will never forget. Somehow I know Mum was laughing right along with us.

We were informed a few days later, after the autopsy, that she had slipped quietly away early in the morning of August 1, 2011, from undiagnosed pulmonary atherosclerosis. To this day, I can barely pronounce what was basically a blood clot block in the artery that really needs to be open for the blood to get to the heart. It goes by another name: heart disease. I didn't even know what that was. All I could think was why the heart? She was fifty years old—so young, so vibrant, so full of life. Suddenly, she was no longer here.

This was the moment in my life that woke me up. Nothing would ever be the same, and somehow I knew I didn't want it to be.

I had spent the last nine months blaming the woman I now so dearly wanted to hold in my arms. I knew I was angry with her for something. I had been so busy telling myself all the stories I needed to hear to make it her fault as opposed to mine. All throughout that time I hadn't once thought what if? What if something were to happen today that would prevent me from ever being able to apologize? And that was all I desperately wanted to do from that point forward. I waited years for her to change our relationship with a deep-seated belief that it was her responsibility, as the mother, to fix it. She is the mother, and she should know better.

All I wanted to do was sleep. I just wanted to plant myself in my bed and never come out. I would scream into my pillow as I cried for hours and hours, I'm so sorry Mum, I'm so sorry. Part of me hoped she could hear me, the other part hoped I could hear me.

There was a time when I wondered if I would ever pull myself out of it. I stared at a depression medication prescription beside my bed (again) on the night table waiting to be filled. Why hadn't I filled it? I was urged by a friend to try a therapist and that only lasted a few sessions. It didn't make sense to me to sit there with a stranger and explore the problem so much. I didn't need to understand the problem, and the problem was clear to me. I needed a solution. So, if the solution wasn't drugs, or a therapist, or my bed for hours on end, what was it?

> *"The truth will set you free, but first it will piss you off."*
> —Gloria Steinem

After Mum's funeral I returned to Canada to resume my fragmented life. I desperately wanted to fall back into a thoughtless system I had created so I could move through time and eventually heal myself. I had a few friends who made regular attempts to take me out and get my mind off what was clearly consuming me. I felt they really didn't know how to talk about what had happened. I was just waiting for someone to really ask me how I was feeling so I could let it all out, but they tried their best to remain careful and avoid the topic. They didn't know how to handle me, and I played along like I didn't need to talk about it. We all danced around the elephant in the room, constantly in fear of not being able to handle the emotion that was sure to follow.

On one particular outing with a good friend, we were dancing around the elephant in the room as usual, avoiding the topic of my mum or how I was feeling. I quietly hoped she would ask me how I was feeling and she probably quietly hoped I wouldn't bring it up. After a while there had been some silence between us and she must have realized I was lost in my thoughts, staring off into the distance. Something compelled her to say something, most likely to break the uncomfortable silence. I'm sure it was no more than a passing thought to encourage me to come back into the moment with her, but she said to me, "It's okay, Marn, you will be okay. Everything happens for a reason."

It's funny how such a nonsensical statement—an empty cliché used far too often—could anger me so deeply. I couldn't understand how something so terrible could happen to me for a reason. What possible reason was there for my beautiful mum to be taken away so suddenly at age fifty, before we would resolve our issues and be at peace? What possible reason?

It seemed so insensitive to me; I was exploding with anger on the inside. I didn't let my friend see that what she had so nonchalantly said had upset me almost unreasonably, at least so I thought. But I left that day thinking. What possible reason could there be for so much heartache, loss, and confusion? I didn't know then, but I believe I know now.

It was the truth that I didn't want to hear. It was a long time before I was able to accept what had happened. I was looking to understand in order to heal, but the truth is I may never really understand. I needed to accept. Acceptance was the first part of my healing.

Acceptance became the key to forgiveness. Forgiveness became the key to the freedom I needed to move forward with my life.

I can't change the past. But I can change what's to come, and it starts with me. It had to come from me. This is why the statement didn't make sense at the time. I wasn't ready to hear the truth and accept it at the time. But if it weren't for her nonchalant statement that day I don't know that I would have put it all together the way I eventually did.

Something was ignited in me that day. I felt something other than sadness for a change. I felt charged — albeit negatively, but it was something. It opened up a small crack to let in a new level of awareness. It is an awareness that today I am so grateful for.

What is so surprising about something so tragic is a potential for rebirth.

This was an ending. A big one. And after an ending comes inevitably, a new beginning. As if jolted into a new reality, I knew nothing again. I had lost all the reasons I couldn't change. I couldn't remember all the excuses I had developed for not going after what I truly wanted in life, and I remembered I had a fire symbol tattooed in the middle of my back ten years ago for a reason. Maybe I should have had it tattooed on my forehead.

The first year after my mum left this world was a big emotional blur of dark, unbearable, hazy confusion. I was left undone, I had no way of saying "I'm sorry" or "It was all your fault," one more time. Both of these statements I wanted to say with equal enthusiasm. Yet there were no answers, no apologies, no well wishes, and no chance to tell her how much I love her again. I couldn't see how I was going to pull myself out. Again, for the third time in my life, I was prescribed medication for depression. And for the third time, I didn't open the box.

Somehow I felt it was a choice for me to feel better and yet I just couldn't quite get there. I chose depression. It seemed easier for me to hide in my sadness than having to grow. It seemed easier to feel sorry for myself rather than putting my big girl pants and my superhero cape on.

I was lost. Mostly alone, I told myself the stories of how I got here. I told myself big fancy stories full of blame, regret, anger, confusion, and sadness. I told myself those stories so often that they eventually became the truth. In other words, those stories became beliefs. These beliefs drove my decisions and influenced my actions. I needed to learn something in order to change it all. I just didn't know what.

I believe everything in life is designed to teach us something and, until we learn it, it will continue to show up. After all, everything happens for a reason—sometimes for reasons we can't see right away.

A significant emotional event will trump everything every time. A drastic change in perspective often takes place after a significant emotional event. It can cause you to question what you believe to be true, when suddenly something you didn't think possible has taken place. It's certainly not the way I would recommend changing some of your beliefs, but it's an effective one.

If you want change, you can have it. But you have to be a willing participant.

Part Two:
IT'S NOT YOU, IT'S ME

CHAPTER NINE
Belief is the New Black

9

The Bounce Back

"I always did something I was a little not ready to do. I think that's how you grow. When there's that moment of 'Wow, I'm not really sure I can do this,' and you push through those moments, that's when you have a breakthrough."

—Marissa Mayer

Write stuff down. Trust me.

It was New Year's Eve 2012. The world eagerly anticipating the year 2013. The perception of change at this time of year sparks something in us—perhaps the possibility for change? The belief that things could be different in the passing into a new year. After dragging myself around for too long, I made a decision to pay attention to this spark of possibility. This one decision would be the catalyst to set me on the path for where I am today, even though I didn't know that at the time.

I offered to host a New Year's Eve party in my small messy condo for a few close friends who were in town and looking for something low-key to do. I had decided I wasn't up for much more effort than that anyway. As I was preparing for the event and cleaning up the pigsty I called home, I found a blank journal that was given to me for Christmas by an incredible mentor of mine named Cathy. Cathy was not only my boss at the time, she was also my confidant and my friend, the reason I went to work every day. If it weren't for her, I would have likely given up on myself a long time ago. What she had no way of knowing was that this small token gift was probably one of the most significant moments of change in my life.

I don't know what came over me but I had to write in this journal on New Year's Eve. It felt somewhat symbolic of the spark of possibility I knew was inside me. As I stared at the blank pages, deciding what I wanted to christen the first page with, I knew it had to be something big, something epic that would become the driving force to a transformation I desperately needed to make.

It was in this moment I realized—this was my life. Like the book, my life was just waiting to be designed by me. I could write anything I wanted.

I wanted to write something so profound that every day beyond January 1 I would read it and it would light me up, illuminate the path I needed to walk until I could run. And without any real thought beyond the size of the mission and the impact I wanted it to have on my life, I took out my pen and wrote.

Marnie Kay
2013 Year of the Entrepreneur

There are two things I would like to say about this. First, I'm pretty sure I didn't spell entrepreneur right. Second, I hadn't the faintest idea about how to become an entrepreneur or even what they did really. But it didn't matter. I wanted to be one, whatever it was. It sounded fun and freeing—two of my favorite 'F' words. Also, 'Entrepreneur' was a big enough bucket that I could live out all my passions inside of it which included writing a book (this one), travelling the world and inspiring others. I gave myself some wiggle room as I wasn't entirely sure any of it was possible, yet.

What was interesting about this decision is that it brought forward a desire that until now I had ignored mostly because I was scared of what I didn't know. It was a dream hidden behind a veil of fear. That veil of fear that didn't need to exist because it wasn't real; I had simply made it all up to avoid actually doing anything about it, just in case I failed. I started to wonder, How many other dreams were behind this veil?

Something magical happened when I wrote these few words in my journal that day. I felt empowered for the first time in a long time because it came from within. No one suggested I do it or forced my hand onto the paper. I did it. The thought, the decision, the action: I did all of it.

TWO MAJOR DISCOVERIES happened here...

1. I had found a new level of awareness just by first making a simple decision that I wanted more. BAM! Childlike possibility was back in all its glory. I started to wonder how much more was in there?

2. I found something I wanted to focus on other than the pain. I made the decision to focus on something I wanted more than all the shit I didn't.

So, it's simple, really: what I wrote down that day, the decision I made, increased my awareness and changed what I was focusing on. I started to think about the idea, tell myself some stories of the possibilities (instead of the barriers) that changed how I felt. All of this started to raise my belief in what was possible and diminish any thought or idea that suggested otherwise.

I understand now that this New Year's Eve Decision, as it came to be known, was the result of finally being sick and tired of being sick and tired. I had finally had enough, released this beautiful intention into the universe and what do you know? Abracadabra... poof!

Opportunities started showing up, hard and fast. I jumped on them, wholeheartedly and haphazardly. Was I successful at first? Hell no. But I began to think positively and feel excited about my potential again; I remembered I had some.

I found that spark. The fire inside that I had forgotten I had literally tattooed on the middle of my back. It was there all along;I just pulled that veil away and threw it in the garbage.

Just by changing what I was focused on, I changed my entire outlook on life. I could feel the fire burn through my chest again for the first time since losing my mother at a time in my life when I needed her most. I was learning instead that I needed myself more. This was the beginning.

AWARENESS CHANGES EVERYTHING.

CHAPTER TEN
Belief is the New Black

10

Advance to Go, Collect $200

IN MY DARKEST MOMENTS OF FEAR I HAD SOMETHING TO LEARN. In my brightest moments of accomplishment I had something to learn. What I have learned thus far is that I'll never stop learning. This is the beautiful thing about life; it is a classroom available to us at all times to grow and become the person we are supposed to be. If we aren't there yet, there are two ways we can make a drastic change to our beliefs and therefore the outcome.

One is a traumatic emotional event. This was my way. I don't want it to be your way but that's up to you. The other is to make a decision (like I did eventually) that you want more and that you are willing to go to work on holding yourself accountable to that decision.

The decision starts with a new awareness. It starts with changing the way you think.

So let's begin here. If I were to say you could have anything you want just by first believing you can, you probably wouldn't believe me. You'd be right in one sense, some work is involved—often a lot of work. But where I challenge you to think differently is that belief is weaved through the tapestry of everything we think, say, and do. Success in anything —whether it is relationships, money, or career— is ultimately impossible without some positive, empowering beliefs along the way. It is not merely a belief that what you want is possible but, in fact, inevitable.

Success of any kind has everything to do with belief, just not necessarily in the way you might think.

The most successful people in the world would tell you they first had to believe they could achieve what they did and then their success was inevitable and a rite of passage. If they didn't believe at first, they persisted with focus and action towards a burning desire until they did. Belief makes it a done deal; the results just catch up with persistence toward the goal.

To demonstrate an example of this, go back to when you were

short stuff, a mere spec on the world, open to anything, excited and in a constant state of awe and wonderment. This place of innocent ambition for me meant I was going to be a doctor, a lawyer, and a famous Hollywood actor like Marilyn Monroe. There was no question about it. Why? Because, in my eyes, anything was possible. We hadn't learned all the reasons why we couldn't do something yet. We hadn't learned all the rules of the game made up by society and culture— people no smarter than we are, as Steve Jobs has so eloquently stated. We were just being aware of our potential.

As children, we just went about our days creating an image in our minds that anything is possible, until we learned otherwise. And we do learn otherwise.

As adults I believe the closest thing to that feeling of reckless abandon we felt as kids is the experience of falling in love. That same state of just being is illuminated when we feel love. It's like when we were specs with our capes on, love compels us to abandon the rules, let go of inhibitions, and go with the wind. Love is beautiful, carefree, and all encompassing.

It's in this state that possibility comes alive. Anything is possible again.

Unfortunately, it doesn't always last. Whether the relationship itself ends or not, the love can fade. And, if it does, we forget almost instantly everything that came with it. The lack of inhibition seems almost cringe-worthy now. What happened when that feeling of love was gone? Usually you learn something, right? Maybe you learned a new belief about relationships? Maybe you cemented a belief into truth that had only been an idea up until now? Add that to your inventory of limiting beliefs, you might need it one day to justify why it doesn't work next time around.

And all the possibility that was there in the state of love? Gone. With the same wind that brought it in.

And then off you go again, back out into the world with a few more beliefs in the bonnet. You're a little more cautionary this time because now you know that men are all assholes. It's really tough to find a good guy, you might say. And the fact that he didn't message you back within fifteen minutes means he probably cheated on you. It's possible that he was in the shower, but it's more likely he cheated on you. And you came to this conclusion because, let's face it, if he really cared he would have taken the phone into the shower with him just in case you messaged so that he was ready to respond instantly.

My point here is that there is no inherent meaning in anything other than that which we give it, or to the extent we are aware.

Have you ever been wrong in an assumption you had made that you were sure was the truth? I certainly have. Is it possible, then, that you could be wrong now?

I had been married at one point in my life, but it ended. After it dissolved I spent some time alone. All I wanted was to be happy with myself, by myself, and to know I hadn't lost myself. After some time I began to feel energy again, unattached to all the stories I had tied to the marriage and why it wasn't working. Someone I had known for some time through friends came into my life romantically for the first time. I hadn't once considered it prior to that moment, perceiving him as egotistical and obnoxiously loud. I had usually been more attracted to the quiet artsy type; maybe I had typically been the egotistical, obnoxiously loud part of the relationship and there was only room for one.

We found ourselves in the same place at the same time with friends. Being in a different place emotionally, maybe I was more open to his ego. We had a conversation… about me. This was strange to me, almost uncomfortable. It had been so long, I thought, since someone was totally interested in me. He told me I was idealistic (a word I didn't fully understand at the time), and that was wonderful. This began our short-lived lively relationship. Maybe two overbearing egos was too much.

I believed he could challenge me, inspire me to become

my best. He was driven, intellectually smart, and passionate about surprising me and making me happy. Yet all of this was fueled with the same fire that ended the relationship abruptly. He became possessive and controlling, and I pulled away. This made him confused and angry. So I pulled away more. Ultimately, I called it all off; he begged me to stay but I was so disengaged at this point, there was no return.

He became so controlling toward the end, all I wanted to do was run away and pretend the whole thing never happened. I couldn't believe I could end up in such a relationship. I had only seen such things in the movies and didn't believe it would really happen to me. I felt like I was in a movie, playing a helpless character stuck in a relationship based on fear. I didn't know what he would do, what he was capable of, but I knew enough to know I had to get out before I found out.

I have had about five relationships that were somewhat serious—involving a future together. Only one of which wasn't ended by me. It would be silly of me to think this obvious trend wasn't somehow connected to my childhood and a belief I have about relationships. Honestly, I believe relationships aren't intended to be a prison. Sure there are ups and downs and good times and challenging times, but if two people are no longer prioritizing each other and the connection, it's okay to move on. This could be a limiting belief of mine in that I am limiting my ability to mend or solve the problem that the relationship is in. Either that or I am simply unwilling to try.

In retrospect, if I didn't have those experiences and make those decisions, I wouldn't be where I am today—limiting belief or not. It doesn't mean I have to continue believing this now that I am aware of it. In fact, I probably have more tolerance for the challenging times than ever before. This just provides me with options in future challenges. I can choose the result, the meaning, and the story. And so I do.

Our beliefs are an amalgamation of thoughts, memories, and ideas imposed upon us by a variety of contributors, corroborated by you and what you focus on.

Seldom do we stop to question if our beliefs are our own or someone else's. Yet everyone and everything you have been exposed to in your life has played a role in the beliefs you have today. Your awareness of this simple fact will allow you to start to question some of what you just know to be true.

Let's take a look at a basic example. Think back to some of the sayings you heard as a child. These are the sayings that, if you asked your parents what it actually meant they would probably have to make something up on the spot in order to try and answer you intelligently. For example, here are some things that I heard when I was a child.

"Wipe that look off your face; if the wind changes, it'll stay that way."

"Money is the root of all evil."

"Don't crack your knuckles; you'll get arthritis."

These are obviously silly examples, but you can see how something so simple can impact our lives in a big way—probably not the wind or the knuckles, but you get my point. The money belief has absolutely played a role in my life, albeit an unconscious one.

The beliefs we have carried on through generations, culture, social settings, and experiences are also the reason why we are where we are in life, and why have what we have.

Where you are in life and what you have is simply the result of the underlying beliefs you hold.

Our beliefs are the foundation upon which our world is created.

Through our words and our behaviors our beliefs play out physically and are reflected back to us in the world around us. Silently and aloud we are expressing these moment by moment, often unconsciously in the decisions we make, who we spend time with, and how many times a day we think to ourselves, Why me?

I know you do it because I do it, too. Bob Proctor, legendary speaker from the hit movie The Secret, author of You Were Born Rich, and world-renowned success coach, taught me to "study yourself and you'll soon understand how everyone else works." Why? Fundamentally when you get past culture, we are all the same.

My thoughts on our beliefs, in agreement with many thought leaders I have studied on the subject, are that they are generalizations about the world and how it all works. Our beliefs come from two major influences: genetics and environment. They come from personal experience, habitual stories (both ours and other people's), dogma and doctrine—what our parents and significant role models told or showed us was fact.

Your life reflects your beliefs; it's not the other way around. They are internal convictions that we hold onto and attempt to prove as fact because, as humans on the search for significance, we have an inherent need to be right. We build up evidence around us to prove that our ideas and our beliefs are right.

If we are right then we are in control. We know what we can count on which gives us a sense of certainty.

So, if our beliefs are an amalgamation of ideas, thoughts, and stories, then how do we know which way is up? How can we determine the real Prada from the knock off version sold on Canal Street, in the beautiful city of New York?

The answer is AWARENESS.

But before we open the doors to the magic kingdom of Nordstrom's, you need to first be aware that Nordstrom's exists. Shopping in general was an amazing, soul-satisfying experience until the day you found out about Nordstrom's. Suddenly, shopping anywhere else was second rate and nowhere near the bench that Nordstrom's has created. Your awareness has been expanded. Now you know there is more to life.

Becoming aware of our thoughts and the imaginative stories we tell ourselves is both exciting and terrifying.

TRY THIS ON.

Picture yourself walking inside the front door of Nordstrom's with a limitless credit card and finding out you need a PIN code to use it. In order for you to be able to purchase anything you have to clear your mind of every single negative thought. By clearing your mind of negative thoughts, you will have access to the card. Every negative thought that creeps in instantly changes the PIN code on the card. You want to purchase what you see and you know you can, but you just have to remain totally positive. The second a negative thought creeps in, the PIN code changes again.

Sounds frustrating? Welcome to your brain! It has to leap to every thought you have all day, every day. Good, bad, ugly: it simply works to reinforce everything you think. You have to be right, remember?

To use your limitless credit card, you need to think only positive thoughts of gratitude, possibility, happiness, and love. Just try it. Pretend you hold that credit card in your hand. Close your eyes; you are standing in the middle of Nordstrom's and the PIN will be handed to you after you have remained positive for at least five consecutive minutes.

Set a timer to go off in exactly five minutes. Close your eyes and think only positive, completely empowering thoughts. Ready? Go! How did you go? Didn't happen? Did something gross pop in? You remembered something your boss said to you that totally pissed you off and then what you should have said in response but you didn't quite think of it on the spot? You never seem to have a good enough response at the time and this is probably why he picks on you. And you're done; Hand the credit card over; there's the door.

That was only five minutes out of your day, not a long time. It was difficult, right? Even with a dangling cupcake (a.k.a. carrot) we struggle to keep the mind totally focused on the positive and that's just while you're thinking about thinking. That's just when you're being in the moment, totally aware of what's happening in your mind.

Imagine when you're not thinking about thinking the other

twenty-three hours and fifty-five minutes of the day.

On the one hand, you now know you can think about thinking, which is the magic of the evolution of the human race and an amazing new awareness for you. We are the only species on the planet with this ability. We can think about what we think about.

On the other hand, you now know you have the power to change it, which means you are the only problem you'll ever have. And the only solution.

"We cannot change what we are not aware of, and once we are aware, we cannot help but change."
—Sheryl Sandberg

Welcome to a New Awareness.

CHAPTER ELEVEN
Belief is the New Black

11

Self-Sabotage: How's That Working for You?

WE ALL DO THE SELF-SABOTAGE THING. We tend to start when we're very young. One of the most difficult times in our lives is becoming a young adult. Stuff just doesn't make sense. So we try to make it make sense in our heads with stories of reasons and justifications. The world is seemingly working against you while you try to feel good about yourself and what lies ahead, you are clouded in confusion and a million different messages, suggesting there are more problems than solutions. Around the age of thirteen we are in a way warned by the world and the media to get ready for high school—a place rife with drugs, gangs, sex, and drama.

I didn't get a warning. I wasn't allowed to watch these TV shows or movies. I didn't even get a conversation. I was handed a book about puberty and a box of tampons. The media, TV shows, movies, and even our role models and parents all start to become really involved in our lives. We are looking for answers about what we've signed up for and we find them, or at least our version of them. The roller coaster of hormones and rules, neither of which make much sense to a thirteen-year-old, becomes the time in our lives when we start to really form beliefs about how things work and who we are.

The stories we tell ourselves become the only thing that makes sense, all because we are looking for answers and we think we have them.

Where we look for the answers will determine what beliefs we come away with. And now, with social media literally in our pockets, we have more answers than we even have the questions for. We know about sex long before we know about puberty. We have images of what beautiful is before we know how to apply mascara. We are handed a brochure in the form of an iPhone as we enter our teenage years, informing us of life's coming attractions.

Facebook, Instagram, magazines, and television: it all comes with a giant firetruck-sounding alarm suggesting urgency and importance.

Congratulations! You're heading into puberty! Batten down the hatches! You're about to become a complete mixed bag of unexpected emotions. Things aren't going to make sense most of the time. Your best friends turn out to be your worst enemies. You can count on being confused, lost, sad, hurt, hysterically in love with someone who doesn't even know your name, cheated on, loved deeply by people you don't know exist. You'll want for more than you have, feel insanely jealous or hurtfully critical. You'll be a bitch, a tease, a monster you don't even recognize, a drama queen, a loose cannon. Okay, take a deep breath.

You'll be a klutz, have "dumb blonde" moments (even if you're not blonde). You'll be both a fashion queen and a fashion disaster. You'll hate the mirror, love the mirror. You'll be a selfie-taking, smack-talking, money-hungry, burger-loving, beer drinking, attention-seeking, Facebook-addicted ball of emotions who is kind of pretty, maybe a bit skinny, sometimes fat, too tall for boys, too lost for girls, and otherwise not that smart…

I think by now you get the point.

What then takes place, as all of this unfolds externally and internally is confusion and fear resulting in the stories we tell ourselves to make it all make sense. Those stories become the beliefs we have picked up and cemented into our unconscious mind.

It's these stories that form the beliefs that we operate from consciously and unconsciously for the rest of our lives, until we decide to tell a different story.

What a shocking time in our lives to develop beliefs and decide what we are capable of or not capable of. In fact, the worst thing we can do is suggest any information on what this time of life should look like. This simply limits us on what is possible. A little bit of information or some stories from someone else, a magazine article or a movie can ruin you.

These stories are simply someone's version of the truth. The more conviction that someone has, or the more you are beaten over the head with it, the more you believe it. Next thing you know it's your story and it then becomes your belief.

A belief that has a butterfly effect on the rest of your life.

Sarah Silverman, a very successful comedian, writer, and actress has said, "Stop telling girls they can be anything they want when they grow up. I think it's a mistake. Not because they can't, but because it would have never occurred to them they couldn't."

What and who we are surrounded by when we are growing up is what shapes us. Whether it's encouragement or fear we develop beliefs about ourselves based on what we learn from the world around us. We are now the most socially connected generation on the planet, so avoiding hearing anyone's version of anything would only be possible if you lived in a box underground with no connection to the outside world. Good luck. I was fourteen once for a year. It was tough (and that was without Facebook!). But I managed, came out with a few high school scars, some emotional wounds but I lived to tell the tale. And so can you.

Even if you could have finished high school five times over again by now, so can you.

The smallest things can shape what we think and, in turn, what we believe.

One particularly memorable experience took place in my magical fourteenth year of life, my second year of high school. I received a note on my desk, passed to me by who I deemed to be the hottest boy in school—I'll just refer to him as Hot Boy from now on. Hot Boy winked at me as I picked it up; I'm sure he could tell by my face that I was excited to read it, and he was obviously about to profess his undying love for me. I proceeded to read the page as I contained my stomach butterflies waiting for the moment that all of my greatest desires would be realized..

I opened the note. "Can I ask you a question?" the note read. My heart was pounding as I looked back at Hot Boy, who was grinning from ear to ear.

I continued to read: "If you didn't have feet, would you wear shoes?"

I look back at Hot Boy slightly confused. This isn't what I was expecting to read, I thought, but I shook my head and mouthed the word "No." I couldn't help but giggle a bit. Obviously I wouldn't wear shoes if I didn't have feet! This must be funny joke or something to get my attention. Then, out of the corner of my eye, I notice yet another note heading in my direction. Okay, this is it, I thought. Hot Boy was still grinning.

I open it up and… I stop breathing. My heart pounded as I heard giggling behind me. Don't look back, I told myself. Oh God. This is embarrassing. I filled up with a special kind of hurt; tears welled up in my eyes.

"Then why do you wear a bra," the second note read. That amounted to immediate social suicide.

Needless to say at this point but I didn't have any boobs when I was fourteen. I mean I obviously had boobs but, compared with my friends, I looked like I should have been about five years younger, or a boy. I was very much into sports and had never thought twice about my body or my boobs. I wore a bra because all my friends did. I had to beg my mum to buy me a flimsy little training bra that she didn't think was even necessary at the time. I had never really thought about my lack of lady lumps until this day, because it just wasn't an issue for me.

Instigated by Hot Boy in grade 9 and for more years than I care to admit I ran the story through my mind that my boobs aren't big enough. When I was fifteen I skillfully skipped school one day to travel by train to a doctor's office armed with a friend's medical card (and her permission). I wasn't feeling ill and I had no real health concerns. I just had one question, one simple question that I had been building up the courage to ask a medical professional: "Do you think my boobs are going to get any bigger, or is this it?"

It seems funny to me now that I desperately needed to know the fate of my future breast growth for which a walk-in doctor really has no way of knowing the answer. I remember her response like it was yesterday. She knew I wasn't the person named on the medical card but she played along, thankfully. She peered over her reading glasses, casually shrugged at my question and said, "Probably not. Maybe a little, but probably not."

It was as I had expected. Doomed to a life with small boobs, I slowly dragged myself back to the train station to take myself home for the day. I pondered what my life might be like with this daunting news.

You have to admire the ability we have to create a reality. One small experience ignited the idea; by focusing on it, the internal dialogue made it larger, more important and, ultimately, true.

I went to work on burning this idea into my unconscious by building up evidence from those around me. I compared myself to other girls, magazines, and models just to make it all true. Once it was true in my mind, I was vindicated in feeling sorry for myself, quietly doomed to forever compare my B-cup to the rest of the women in the world.

That one otherwise harmless joke caused an all-consuming belief about myself that resulted in a severe body image issue. I began stuffing my bra with tissues, avoided swimming in public (previously one of my favorite things to do). I even went so far as to starve myself, thinking my boobs would look bigger if I were slimmer. It's amazing how creative we can get to accommodate our made-up beliefs and reinforce the stories we tell ourselves.

Body image issues today are more prevalent than ever before or, at least, they are more exposed. We have more in-your-face comparisons available at our fingertips with social media. As a result we have higher expectations of ourselves just to keep up or fit in.

It's no wonder we have staggering mental health concerns today. When I was fifteen, to scrutinize and compare my boobs I would have to almost obviously stare at my friend's chest or get my hands on an inappropriate magazine. Today you can Google that stuff all day long and no one would ever know you were quietly sinking into despair.

The stories we tell ourselves are both the justification and the convincer. The more you tell them to yourself, the more it's the truth. Repetition is a powerful thing.

It's a slippery slope. One story leads to another and another. Before you know it you have full-blown, irreparable self-esteem issues. And then we take it up a notch.

As adults, we are no longer competing for an invitation to a party or a Hot Boy's attention. It becomes a competition with your own worst enemy, your harshest critic, your internal bitch. And she doesn't sleep. This bitch works twenty-four hours a day, seven days a week, 365 days a year. I call her Betty.

And she will not rest until you stop paying attention to her. Betty is the voice inside your head that runs the stories, chatters all day long, and plays on your limiting beliefs over and over again. Let's all say hello to Betty.

CHAPTER TWELVE
Belief is the New Black

Introducing Betty, Your Internal Bitch

"Tell the negative committee that meets inside your head, to sit down and shut up."
—Ann Bradford Davis

TRY THIS ON:

Play with me here for a moment. Throw your hands in the air enthusiastically if you have ever uttered the following either out loud or in your head...

I wish I looked like her

He/she would never date someone like me

I'm not good enough for him/her/that job/that dream

I wish I had more time/money/love/shoes

He/she probably won't call me anyway

I am fat today/everyday/in general

I could go on for days, making an entire book consisting of the stories we tell ourselves. But I'll stop here and get to the point.

We like certainty. We like to know things for sure.

At the end of the day, all of this is a protection strategy to keep us at a safe distance from failing or getting hurt (i.e. pain). After all, it probably won't work out anyway right?

Betty (as I like to call her), your newfound friend, is that voice that prepares you, warns you for what will probably happen, scolds you for making a mistake, convinces you of why something didn't work out, and justifies everything for you, in a nice little negative, repetitive box called your mind.

The bad news is this bitch, Betty, is on a mission and she won't stop until you show her she is irrelevant and unnecessary. She is out to sell you on the worst stories, sabotage you before you even begin, and keep you in a safe place where only she can get to you. So why do we listen to our own versions of Betty?

Why do we give her airtime or allow her to repeat the negative thoughts and limiting beliefs over and over? Why would we knowingly infiltrate our beautiful powerful minds with disempowering thoughts and beliefs?

I've done a lot of study and searching these past few years for the answer to that question. Why do we continue to hang onto these old limiting beliefs instead of going after what we want? Why does Betty live wild and free in our minds to lead the charge on the storytelling? Of everything I have studied, I have come to believe there are four main reasons WHY we listen to Betty and accept the limiting beliefs we've created, deciding to live a life less than we are meant for. Get some popcorn and get ready to reflect on your own life and the choices you have made as a result of these four ideas.

1. SAFETY—We work hard to protect ourselves from failing or getting hurt. Once we have been hurt or we have failed at something we create a belief around it. Then we work hard to build evidence to make it true. This is to keep us insulated from failure. We find comfort and control if we can use these stories and beliefs to predict future results. This is largely fueled by fear and survival, self preservation. Avoid the pain or you get a stick whipping.

For example, you might say, when considering a change at work, "I'm probably too young for that promotion, so I'll wait a few years to apply until I have gathered enough respect from my peers."

2. EGO—We feel good when we can assert ourselves, project an identity, and express who we are by making a stand. Born out of a need to feel significant and fueled by fear of lack of significance. We need to feel needed, important and loved.

For example, "I don't want the promotion right now; I'm focused on other things."

3. ACCEPTANCE — To feel included, we will adapt and conform to a common belief to 'join the pack.' We want to be a part of something, feel connected. We will often adopt certain beliefs to fit in especially with family and friends.

For example, "I agree Sally should get the promotion; she has a lot of respect in the company."

4. JUSTIFICATION — This is when we reason to understand. We label it as something that makes sense so we can feel vindicated and right. Also known as 'certainty'.

For example, "I know they like Sally more than me, so she will probably get the promotion."

The problem with these four 'reasons'; safety, ego, acceptance and justification is that you if ever want to be successful, run your own business, lead an empire, love yourself, or take risks and have no regrets at the end of it all, you have to at some point abandon or push through them.

Ditch Betty and leave her in the dust. I'm not budging on that bold statement. Feet glued to the floor. Betty must take a back seat, along with these 'reasons'.

The good news is Betty is just an inner voice. She is a voice in your head; you can turn down the volume or turn her off and change the station completely. Now that you are aware of her, you can simply choose to ignore her stories. Or—even better—you can make up another story, one that empowers you instead.

Learn to become aware of Betty and you're halfway there.

When I became aware of Betty I suddenly became aware of how I was so accustomed to her being there; I was used to this conversation I was having with myself. I just didn't know any better.

The turning point in my life (where I changed the station on Betty) was that one bold decision on New Year's Eve of 2013, when I asked myself, "What if this isn't it?" and "What if there is more?"

What if what I had been waiting for had been there all along waiting for me?

What if I continued to wait for it so that I could finally choose to be happy?

What If I missed it or let it go because of these stories I tell myself?

What if I'm doing it all wrong?

And, indeed, I was doing it all wrong. I had been carrying so many limiting beliefs with me from my formative years that they literally stopped me from even thinking about what I wanted or deeply desired… let alone going after it.

I will teach you what I did to change it. It's not easy. There are days where Betty drops in to remind me I am human, but I am stronger than ever before now, equipped with the tools that I continue to practice to become the person I want to be. So, it's time to let Betty know, "We are coming for you; your time is up!"

CHAPTER THIRTEEN
Belief is the New Black

13

Gradually, We Realize We Had It All Along

"Something amazing happens when we surrender and just love. We melt into another world, a realm of power already within us. The world changes when we change. The world softens when we soften. The world loves us when we choose to love the world."

—Marianne Williamson

I've been hammering in the nail here on the stories we tell ourselves. Why am I doing this? Simply because it is the crack in the armor of our beliefs. This is our way in, to change them! Now that we are aware, it's about making the decision to do something about it.

Which feels better: to be powerless or powerful?

By understanding you are in control of creating whatever beliefs you want, you'll realize just how powerful you are.

Like most people who feel stuck at some point in their lives, this was my mother for many years. In fact, this is most likely where I learned how to be 'stuck' too. I used to listen to all the reasons why she wasn't happy and why none of it was in her control. She was powerless; she would blame the circumstance instead of doing something about it.

She loved the people she worked for, but they didn't pay her enough. She wanted to be more than just a receptionist, but her company didn't have anything to offer. Nonetheless, she was the best receptionist they had. She wanted to meet a great man who loved her unconditionally and would take care of her, but she dated losers. These were her stories. The cycle just went on like this and all I could ever think is, I really hope I don't end up like this: unhappy with my life.

One of the saddest parts of her leaving life as we know it so young is that she still had so much she wanted to do. She had so much of her picture left to paint. The only thing that ever stood in her way was her beliefs. All she ever wanted was love and freedom, yet both were available to her all along.

For many years, in my childhood, my mum seemed unhappy, unsatisfied. I knew she was supposed to take pills but I really didn't know what for. I know now that it was depression and she had been diagnosed with bipolar disorder, but I also know there came a point when she stopped taking her medication and seemed happier than ever. She was a roller coaster of emotions. For many years I was, too. I guess it just seemed 'the norm' to me.

As a young child, I often watched her and wondered if this was it. Was life supposed to be so difficult and frustrating, as it seemed to be for her? Would life make me sad enough to hide in my bedroom all day? Would I leave relationships and jobs and head off in the hunt for something better? I sure hoped not. But the truth was I would do all of these things, in spite of my mission to not follow in her footsteps.

Unsatisfied with life's situations such as my job, success, relationships, and overall happiness, I constantly looked for more, just as she had done before me.

It wasn't until later in life that she found a new happiness with this search, a new comfort in the life she already had. My mum became a beautiful, confident woman who was excited about life again.

On one hand, I love that she was always looking for more. I believe I found a connection in that part of her. Her search for more gave me permission to look, too, not merely to settle or accept what was. And, in hindsight, I wouldn't be where I am today if I didn't follow her lead with the same belief that I could do more, be more, and have more.

But the part that I didn't want was the unhappiness, the

deep sadness of her earlier years, for which I thought us kids were to blame. Could my life today have come without the same pain and sadness? I don't know. But I do know that what was once 'I hope I don't end up like that' is now a part of me that made me who I am. For that I am grateful.

Susan Scott, the fabulous author of Fierce Conversations, stated that "Everything happens gradually then suddenly."

Take a moment to think about everything that has taken place in your life that was seemingly sudden. Now think about where that sudden result may have originated. What could have kick-started the gradual lead-up to the sudden thing that happened?

Without fail, you can almost always trace it back to what was gradually happening until the suddenness showed up, every time.

So, if everything is always happening gradually, then we are much more in the drivers seat than we know. Let's use an example. Health concerns: they are seemingly sudden and always gradual. Bad nutrition, lack of exercise, and little sleep: these all gradually build up to a problem. The diagnosis might come as sudden shock; however, the process of disease or ill health is entirely gradual.

If you have ever lost your job, either by lack of performance or cutbacks, you may be tempted to think this is sudden. What about credit card debt? A relationship breakup? All of these are examples of things that seem sudden when they are, in fact, gradual.

What I take from Susan's idea is not that everything is happening around us gradually but, more poignantly, that we are often moving through life completely unaware of our surroundings, living outside of the moment. Consequently, we don't know it's happening until it has happened already.

Have you ever arrived home at night after work or an outing realizing you cannot actually remember the entire drive? Have you ever finished reading a page of a book realizing you didn't actually take in a single word you read? Think back to a vacation you took where you can only really remember the bits for which you have photos?

Don't worry; you are not alone in this because we all do it. We travel through life so often on autopilot, going through the motions of what looks and feels like activity, without much real thought about it.

It's this lack of awareness and presence that gives power to the stories we tell ourselves. We only see what we want to see.

Think about it. If you aren't present and aware of every moment then what are you basing your stories on? It's highly likely that you have based them on fragmented distortions or generalizations of what actually happened, or a made-up idea of what could happen. And, guess what? That's probably what just took place.

Let's explore this awareness (or lack thereof) further. If you aren't present or in the moment, then you are most likely one of two other places...

1. Hanging out in the past, where we have been. You are probably reliving it, feeling the emotions of it, rolling around in that old dirty blanket. The comfort of it is just soooooo familiar. Playing around with all the evidence to corroborate your story, you justify why you're in this situation. You blame some people or situations, the world, to try and make it all make sense.

2. Or you are off in the future, worrying or in fear about what might happen, how it could get worse, so that you are prepared and ready when it hits, because it's definitely going to. You really should be planning for all the worst possible situations now. Being prepared means you can probably handle it better when it happens. (Right?)

These two familiar stories are the reason the large majority of the population is unhappy. Let's face it: this dirty-blanket-lovin' is the reason our pets are happier than we are. I have a small adorable Chihuahua named Foxie. She has zero concerns in the world other than when I leave my home. Until then my absence doesn't even enter the realm of possibility for her. She lives in a constant state of unconditional love, excitement, and fun. She doesn't live in constant fear of when I might leave the house. However, if it does happen, she deals with it. This is how we should live. I look up to my little pup. She knows how to live the good life.

Humans? We do this all wrong. We love the stories, the reasons, and the noise! We love to sort it all out in our minds and make it make sense.

We are our own commentator keeping the game alive, having a little chat with ourselves all day, every day. It's this noise, the stories and our dear friend Betty on repeat that keep us from being aware, present, in the moment, and grateful.

TRY THIS ON.

Let's play around with this. Imagine having zero concerns, absolutely no worries at all. Imagine then that something does happen and you just deal with it. That's right, just deal with it in the moment. Imagine if you never thought about paying a bill until the moment you received the letter in the mail and then you paid it?

Imagine if you never thought about having to go to work, until the time came and you just got in the car and went? Imagine if you never thought about what you might argue about with your significant other today, what they might do or might not do that annoys you.

Sounds peaceful, quiet even, doesn't it? It's in this quiet space that you can create magic. Both by not running your stories and beliefs constantly and by implementing simple moment-to-moment gratitude for what you have and where you are going.

After all, you do have a choice about what you think about, right?

By getting rid of the negative stories, the limiting beliefs, and replacing them with positive future stories, empowering beliefs, and a vision of where you are going, you can change your entire life.

"The real meaning of a word is only as powerful or as harmless as the emotion behind it."
—Sarah Silverman

Belief is the key or the killer. The beauty is you get to choose. By choosing positive stories, empowering beliefs, and a vision of where you are going, you hold the key to the life you want.

By holding onto the negative stories, giving in to limiting beliefs and replaying the past, belief is the killer. The worst kind.

Beliefs (both empowering and limiting) need you to believe in and reinforce them to have any power or strength. So commit to the one that feels better.

It's a choice we must practice constantly until it becomes unconscious. It's like learning how to drive: just because you have the knowledge of how to start the car, put it in gear, and go in reverse does not mean you have any skill getting that big hunk of metal within the lines, even if you can operate it going backward. In fact, all knowledge and no practice can lead to frustration, anger, and... accidents! Just ask any parents who are teaching their children how to drive. It's the same in practicing the power of belief.

Belief is a skill that needs awareness, practice, and constant focus. The secret is... it's all about what you choose to focus on.

What you focus on is what you get.

CHAPTER FOURTEEN
Belief is the New Black

14

The Cupcake vs the Stick

THERE IS A PLETHORA OF SELF-HELP BOOKS, motivational speakers, and seminars in the world today, all preaching the benefits of thinking positively. They all share the same message: our thoughts and the stories we tell ourselves are our choice. We have control. They encourage us to choose the good thoughts and get rid of the crap.

And it's all about what you focus on.

Focus is a powerful thing, and we absolutely have control over it. It's like a magnet. If you focus on positive things and look on the bright side of life, you're probably a fairly happy person. For the most part positive things show up for you. If, however, you are focusing on shit all the time, then you're probably in trouble. Shit-magnet kind of trouble.

Let's look at some regular examples of how this works. Remember a time when a close friend or family member became pregnant? It's as if somebody spiked the water with embryos (and you could get pregnant by swallowing embryos), everyone is pregnant? Suddenly there's baby stuff everywhere, and you can't get away from it. It's like being pregnant became contagious like the common cold.

Have you ever shopped around looking to purchase a new car? I'll use my new black Jeep as an example. I had rarely seen a Jeep on the roads in my life, much less a black one, before the day I picked mine up. Then, all of a sudden, it's as though there are black Jeeps everywhere! Everyone owns one and I was the last to know. It's like I was the butt of a big Jeep joke and I was missing the punch line.

As we move through this chapter and begin to explore the nature of focus, I want you to remember you have a choice. You choose what you focus on. Once you have awareness of your thoughts you can start interrupt them and change them. . .

Why would you want to change what you are focusing on? Well, in the words of a great teacher of mine, Gina Mollicone-Long, looking at your current situation… "How's that working for you?"

Knowing you need to do something is one thing; actually doing that something is another. You can read all the self-help books and gain all the knowledge in the world. But all the knowledge in the world won't help you if you do nothing with it.

Change requires action. Now that's scary.

In a big world, with television, social and traditional media, movies, society, and even our relationships, it's almost impossible to go any stretch of time without being exposed to something negative. Chances are good that you will either encounter something negative or you'll encounter something that leads you to a negative thought that will trigger a negative story you tell yourself in your mind. This is a story you have probably told yourself before to make something make sense. Now it's on repeat.

Tell yourself something often enough and it will become the truth.

Pay attention to the media or television in the next few days; how much of it is suggesting something negative or has the potential to be viewed as negative? After all, if it's not directly negative, we have an incredible way of taking it there.

Let's use an example. (I love examples!)

Let's start with something seemingly positive.

Setting the Scene:

You see an advertisement for a beach vacation in the Bahamas.

Ooooh, that looks nice, you think, I'd love to go on vacation! I really haven't been on a vacation or a holiday in a long time.

Oh I wish I had enough money to book at least a week away somewhere hot, although I probably shouldn't have gone shopping last weekend—yikes my credit card debt is becoming outrageous. I feel like I can never get it down and I'm just barely paying the interest right now, I'm so stuck! I'm just not happy with my life right now. How did I end up here?

END SCENE.

Sound familiar? And this was a simple vacation advertisement we probably see every day or are even signed up for in our email subscriptions.

[6]Freudian psychology suggests as humans there are two major motivators. Instinctively we seek pleasure and avoid pain in order to satisfy our biological and physical needs.

We seek pleasure and we seek to avoid pain.

For the purpose of this book, and for the sake of having a little fun, let's call it the cupcake versus the stick (because carrots are for horses). Pleasure = the cupcake (obviously) and pain = the stick. According to our stories and assumptions, as well as an emotional viewpoint of both based on experiences, we make decisions every

6 C. R. Snyder and J. Shane. The Handbook of Positive Psychology.

day to either focus on moving toward pleasure or away from pain. While both are powerful motivators, driving away from pain is often the stronger impulse. It is an emotionally charged motivation associated with previously experienced pain, more of which we would do anything to avoid.

In pain, we search for the reason why. I did this after my mum died. I needed to understand why. Why her and why me? I needed to put it in a box and label it because I thought if I had some sort of certainty, that this would help me finally let it go. As long as I didn't understand it I hung onto it and replayed the story to try and make sense of it.

It is not logic that fuels our response to pain; it's the very thing that created it, emotion.

And here begins a nice little (or big honking) negative loop of experience, pain, belief, emotion. This loop can be devastating and completely debilitating. So how do you know whether you are motivated by pain or pleasure? Which one are you focused on? It's simple. How do you feel? If you don't feel good, then you are probably making decisions and are motivated by pain or the avoidance of any further pain. You are driven to get away from the negative, which is in fact a negative drive. Let's call this the Killer. Focusing on pain or the avoidance of pain limits you and your potential. You live in a perpetual state of fear. Very little can be accomplished here, if anything at all.

Alternatively, if you do feel good then you are probably making decisions and operating from pleasure—moving toward what you want and feeling good. This is a positive drive. Let's call this the Key. Focusing on the pleasure increases your limits. It's like falling in love: everything becomes possible once again.

Both are powerful, and the beauty is you get to choose. So which do you choose? Is it the key or the killer? The cupcake or the whipping stick?

CHAPTER FIFTEEN

Belief is the New Black

15

The Dirty Blanket Syndrome

LET'S LOOK AT BELIEF AS THE KILLER.

Again, the negative stories we tell ourselves are what kill our dreams. It's straight up rain on your wedding day, fart on your first date; it's the red wine spill on a white dress, dream-killer.

We all run many versions of these dream killer stories and a lot more unconsciously than we even realize. This is not good. These are destructive stories that need to find an old empty shoe box and climb in and die.

It is stories like these that we unconsciously run that play as a convincer. It's a big dirty old familiar blanket that just feels so comfortable, you want to lie down on it and have a good cry. There's something irresistible about a cozy blanket, right? The blanket understands.

WARNING: *This blanket is your worst enemy. Aside from Betty.*

For me, the dirty blanket was the stories I told myself about why my mum and I didn't have a good relationship. The dirty blanket I rolled around in was the reasons and the excuses that stopped me from doing anything about it for years. It was her fault anyway; that's what I believed, and she should be the one to make it better. She is the mum; she should want to reach out to me. I shouldn't have to push myself into her life. That was indeed one big dirty limiting belief blanket!

If the stories we tell ourselves are toxic, inherent with limiting beliefs that aren't our own ideas for the most part, and all of this is keeping us from discovering our true potential and having a life full of love and abundance, then why do we play them over and over? What purpose does it serve to tell ourselves shit stories that make us feel… like shit?

Why not just choose the good stories?

It's simple really. I think the shit stuff seems more like the truth. Our stories are our version of the facts. We use these stories and our version of what has happened to try and determine what will happen in the future mostly to avoid more pain. That's the stick. Get rid of the stick! Choose the cupcake.

How do you do that? You focus all your energy on the cupcake —

i.e. what you want! Do not give any ounce of energy to what you don't want. It doesn't serve you.

It's time to let go of the dirty old blanket of comfort and run for the hills of cupcakes.

CHAPTER SIXTEEN
Belief is the New Black

16

The Unicorn Affect

NOW LET'S LOOK AT BELIEF AS THE KEY.

When you go to sleep at night and lay your head on the pillow as you fall into a deep slumber, what would you rather have… a dream or a nightmare? A dream, right?

I hope this is your answer. Otherwise, I probably can't help you. Here is the irony and the aha moment. If you would rather have a dream when you are asleep at night filled with riches, people you love, and fun things, then why wouldn't you rather the same thing during the day?

Why not dream full-time and quit the day-mares?

The stories that we tell ourselves of past and present are what give us a feeling of significance (and, trust me, we need to feel significant). They feel real. We have lived it, so the story we have is our version of the truth. But there is almost always more than one version of the same story. This is why lawyers are so highly paid. So if there is more than one version of the same story you can start to see how the truth gets a little shaky here. There are some holes in it. It's not bulletproof.

Yet we maintain these stories as our truth and work really hard to build up evidence around us to support these truths. But we only see what we want to see, and we have an inherent need to be right. So if these truths are constructed about where we have been and where we are now, why not do the same to build your future?

How is the past any more the truth than where you are going?

When I was little girl with big dreams and knee scrapes to match them, I would tell my mother that one day I'll live in Australia for the summer season (October to March) and in America for its summer (April to Sept). This way I will never have to live in the winter and I can swim in the ocean or a pool all year round. I love the water that much.

I believed so much that this would happen with no real plans or thought behind how, all I knew is winter was the worst and I needed to avoid it at all costs. I actually forgot about this little dream of mine until a few years ago. I realized I was actually living it. As it turns out I had the right continent but a little further north than America is where

I landed. I now live between Canada and Australia.

When I moved to Canada eight years ago, I bought a plane ticket thinking Canada was to the east of America, not the north (applause for Australia's education on world geography, or my general lack of interest in geography). I pictured everyone living in igloos with snowshoes, and I thought ice fishing was a national sport. I didn't know that Toronto enjoys a summer as hot as Australia and as humid as the tropics. I absolutely love my multi-continent lifestyle.

Thank you, seven-year-old self, for believing something so wonderful was possible.

This is how belief can be the Key. If you are positive and focused on what you want, your beliefs can enforce your deepest desires and create the world you dream of, even a wonderful story you tell yourself about how you can avoid winter for the rest of your life with no knowledge of how to actually get there.

I also believed in unicorns. I may have watched one too many cartoons, but there was something about unicorns. I think there is for most children. They are the ever-elusive, dreamlike combination of magic and horses. Unicorns are a beautiful creature from a mystical land where princesses and leprechauns live. You can never catch one. I had never seen one but I believed they were out there nonetheless.

I call this the Unicorn Effect. Focus on that unicorn, the wonderful things that you want and dream of, even if you don't know how your wants and dreams can come true. If you can do that you will no longer be running away from something you don't want, such as pain. Instead, you'll be working toward something magical, such as pleasure.

The Unicorn is the pleasure you seek. It's the cupcakes, the Louboutin's, love. Don't let it out of your sight.

We have established by now that our beliefs are learned through experiences and stories. The great thing is anything learned can also be unlearned. As we continue on in this journey of understanding belief, my hope is that you take away a few key strategies on how to change the way you think, to change what you believe and, finally, change what you see in front of you, your life. Or at least your persepctive of it.

You will discover some current limiting beliefs you have that might be keeping you from living the life you want, as well as some positive empowering beliefs that you need to strengthen and reinforce. Finally, you can play some offense and get out of your own way.

You are the only thing in your way, ever.

There are simple things you can do to install positive thoughts and stories and finally move in the direction you want in life. You can move confidently toward your desires (the Unicorn) instead of constantly repelling them away by focusing on what you don't want.

If you can finish this book with a renewed energy for your life and your potential, and feel empowered with some strategies on how to move forward, then I will be forever grateful that this book could play a part in your journey.

Awareness is the first step, focus is what makes it stick. Stop looking at the circular clocks and let's get started!

Belief is both the Killer and the Key.
The beauty is… you get to choose. (HINT: choose the unicorn!)

CHAPTER SEVENTEEN
Belief is the New Black

17
Energy is Everything.
Watch Where You Put It

ONE OF THE BEAUTIFUL PHILOSOPHIES I BECAME FAMILIAR WITH OVER THE PAST FEW YEARS IS AN ANCIENT HAWAIIAN PHILOSOPHY OFTEN REFERRED TO AS HUNA. Huna (the Hawaiian word for 'secret', also said to have been a modern label indoctrinated in the last century) shares the same idea as many religions and cultures today that there is a source of energy, a life force, also known as God. In other cultures such as Chinese or the practise of Tai Chi, it's known as Chi, in the Sanskrit language it's known as Shakti or Prana. The people of Huna, known as Kahuna who practiced these teachings believed seven main principles as they are known and taught today. The origin of Huna is somewhat controversial. Regardless of it's origin, I think it's a pretty cool belief system encompassing spiritual growth through the practical application of seven empowering ideas.

[7]Dr Serge Kahili King, Author of 'Huna: Ancient Hawaiian Secrets for Modern Living', was adopted into this tradition and trained by a family of Huna Heritage on the island of Kauai. Dr King shares the seven principles as a way of empowering oneself.

One of these seven ideas in particular is often shared by the great teacher Tony Robbins in his famous quote 'Where focus goes, energy flows.' and he follows this up with 'And where energy flows, whatever you're focusing on grows. In other words, your life is controlled by what you focus on.'

Known as the third principle of the new age Huna, Makia is 'Energy flows where attention goes'. This is an important idea to understand for the remainder of this book. This is how you give power to your beliefs, limiting or empowering.

The power of our thoughts is also controversial today (what big idea isn't?) but we do know that our energy flows to the thing we are thinking about. Shit magnets, remember? What we focus on is what we find, simply because you are looking for it. It's like deciding you want the latest Celine bag and Poof! that thing is everywhere. You see it featured in magazines. Your friend bought it. Magically it's on your iPad when you didn't intend to shop online this week to save money. It's like they heard you!

This works in harmony with the stories we tell ourselves. Our thoughts, what we choose to think about is what we are focused on. As the story gets bigger in our minds we can't help but focus on it

7 "Huna, Ancient Hawaiian Secrets for Modern Living" by Dr Serge Kahili King www.huna.org, Article Library, The Seven Principles

more. It may feel like you cant help but think about that problem, person or situation. As the story expands and grows in our mind, we feel the need to justify it all, build evidence around it such that it becomes right to further justify the existence of the story in you mind in the first place. Next thing you know your boyfriend is for sure cheating on you with your best friend and everyone knew it but you. And, oh, your boss hates you.

You planted that little seed somewhere along the way and watered the shit out of it. Jack and his giant beanstalk has some competition here.

Knowing now how powerful your focus is, you can understand why all the fuss is around thinking positive. If you think positive then you'll focus on the positive and feel positive as a result. So how do we keep it positive? Thats the hard part!

Trying not to focus on something is like trying not to spill red wine on yourself when you've decided against all better judgment to wear white.

Practically impossible... Or is it?

The amazing thing about the mind is that it will keep running what you are focusing on until you are distracted or make a conscious decision to stop. You can't tell yourself not think about something;

the unconscious mind cannot differentiate between do and do not. It just picks up the thing you think about and runs with it.

TRY THIS ON:

Ready? Okay, don't think about Kim Kardashian.

Impossible right? She's in there now. Even though I said not to think about her. Gotcha!

This is really cool to realize because now you can begin to understand just how powerful you are (in case you didn't already know). Even when you're not looking. So the trick is to catch yourself doing it and change your focus. If you aren't focused on the unicorn, then God knows what can get in there and run amok while you're not thinking about thinking. So you need to catch yourself and switch it with the unicorn, whatever your unicorn is.

Awareness is where you start, but focus is what will carry you over the line.

Janey is a beautiful spiritual friend of mine. We met through a mutual friend who said she was "this really cool chick who sees stuff and reads energy." We quickly became lifelong friends and she has become a great mentor to me. She has taught me how to pay attention and really listen to myself; often I already know the answer. (So do you!)

A few years ago she gave me a yellow candle and suggested I meditate (I stared at her blankly hoping she would explain the word 'meditate' to which she said 'close your eyes and focus'- for now) on the color yellow. I wasn't sure why, she said something about my aura? Either way I wasn't messing around with her spiritual instructions. And at this point I was still fairly new to meditation and how it all worked. I was more concerned about doing it right, even though I didn't know what doing it right was.

Anyway, I went to work. In the bath, on the floor in my condo overlooking the water: I was meditating everywhere. I'd light the yellow candle and focus on yellow things. What I noticed was the more I practiced this with my eyes shut, the more I began to see the color yellow when my eyes were open. I had no idea how many yellow things I had in my apartment until I focused on this yellow candle. I have yellow stuff everywhere. I never noticed because I wasn't looking for it before. Since I began focusing on yellow, it was all I was seeing.

Ask me what's purple in my condo and I couldn't tell you, but yellow? I could list every little thing.

TRY THIS ON:

If you want something to show up in your life, start focusing on it every chance you get. Think about it often, and have a little mantra in your mind; every time you remember say it to yourself. And watch it start to show up all over the place.

REMEMBER:

"Where focus goes, energy flows."
—Tony Robbins

This works whether you are focused on good things or bad things.

Unfortunately for our lives, living 'in the negative' is how we like to generally play the focus game. You know those days where you wake up late, disheveled and slightly annoyed for no apparent reason? It may be one of those days when your hair doesn't work with you, you can't find what you wanted to wear, or you got a message you didn't want to read and its goes on and on from there?

Sometimes we are tempted to say we "woke up on the wrong side of the bed" in those moments. Notice how they get worse and worse as the day goes on? It's almost as if magically the universe decided today that you deserved some shit. Well, in fact, it did, because you did and that's what you have been thinking about.

What you think about shows up like yellow.

The reason we see yellow things, black Jeeps, and the bad stuff we focus on is because our minds cannot possibly consciously retain everything we see. There is simply too much to take in. So our minds unconsciously take screenshots and file everything away for later use. What we do consciously notice and remember is only a very small amount of what is available to us, basically nothing, except for what you are focused on. That's what you're looking for in the first place.

So what does this mean? I said don't think about Kim Kardashian and you can't think about anything but Kim Kardashian. Yellow is everywhere and I'm a shit magnet? Not quite.

(I love Kim, by the way. She is just fabulous and knows it. Belief as the Key right there!)

Your mind runs with or without you on a constant treadmill, and these thoughts and stories played over and over begin to develop a meaning and a feeling associated with the thought or experience. This feeling embeds the belief that it's all tied to. The more you think about and feel all of it emotionally, the stronger it gets—ultimately impacting how you behave and what actions you take.

How you behave very quickly creates the world that's in front you—your relationships, your success. What you see in front of you is simply a result of all that you have thought and believed.

Belief is really just the combination of thoughts fuelled

by feelings. Those feelings are fuelled by thoughts. Somewhere in there you're taking action on what you're thinking about and how you feel, and then all of that starts to show up in your life around you.

For example, if you harbor a nice little limiting belief about your ability in one area of your life, it will generate a negative feeling about that thing in your life.

And then if you aren't feeling good, what are your behaviors?

And if your behaviors aren't good, then what are your results?

And if your results aren't good, then what are you thinking about again?

This is the negative loop of doom. And Betty has been in the driver's seat until now.

TRY THIS ON.

What world have I created with my thoughts and beliefs? And how is it working for me?

These questions, as difficult as it can be to accept at first, are extremely powerful. It helps you do two things…

Acknowledge just how powerful you really are.

Accept responsibility for having created it as well as probably needing to make some adjustments.

Unfortunately, most people live on the cause side of the equation, where you are in the driver's seat. Their world is full of blame and reasons. You don't want to be here. This suggests you are anything but powerful which just isn't true. So by asking these questions you immediately take yourself over to the cause side of the equation, where you are in the driver's seat. Your world is then full of empowerment and options… and much more possibility.

Which side are you on right now? Are things happening to you? Or are you making things happen? Once you truly believe that everything in your life is a result of all that you think, focus on, believe, and do, then you will understand how powerful you really are. Our quality of life is merely a reflection of the quality of our beliefs, what we think about, and what we think we are capable of.

What world have I created with my thoughts and beliefs? And how is it working for me?

If it's not working for you… change it.

"Passion is energy. Feel the power that comes from focusing on what excites you."
—Oprah Winfrey

CHAPTER EIGHTEEN
Belief is the New Black

18

Get a Strategy, Get Results

"You gain strength, courage and confidence by every experience in which you stop to look fear in the face."

—Eleanor Roosevelt

Awareness, focus, unicorns and dirty blankets. So where do we start? Now that you have a better understanding of why all of this is so important and how it works, let's get into what we can do to show Betty who is boss.

After all, Betty is just you standing in your way.

We have a system or program for most things we do in life. From breathing to digesting food, how we respond in a crisis right down to how you shower or tie your shoelaces. Either biological or learned, unconscious or conscious, it's these systems and programs that we use to solve problems, respond to situations and, ultimately, live, develop, and grow.

If you were to cut yourself shaving (an otherwise fairly mundane task), your body will send a signal to clot the cut. This is a survival system we employ unconsciously. Just like when you see your ex-boyfriend in public and would really rather not, your mind springs into action to avoid the situation; the 'avoid ex-boyfriends at all costs' program tells the legs to move and turn the rest of your body, especially your head in another direction, to avoid contact. Contact averted, system of survival at it's best.

Like these programs or systems for survival, we need a simple system in place in order to make positive changes to our lives on a daily basis—the same way we avoid run-ins with ex-boyfriends or save our own lives with blood clots. Here are three basic steps that I employ consistently on a daily basis to build small positive habits every day that have become instrumental in how I work and live.

ENVISION. INGRAIN. ENGAGE

The belief change butterfly! Isn't it beautiful?

The truth is, in order for the butterfly to fly, it first had to crawl as a caterpillar. Like the caterpillar to the butterfly, we evolve also. Here is how you can speed this process up.

ENVISION. INGRAIN. ENGAGE. EIE

This is your mantra. Each as a single strategy and together as a system, provides a framework in which you can build up those beautiful empowering stories and get rid of the crusty old limiting beliefs.

Most people don't have what they really want. They settle because they don't know how to change what they've always done. Here is how you can change.

The three step system ENVISION, INGRAIN, ENGAGE is a series of activities to help you focus on what you want, help you believe you can be, do, have or give it and start working towards what you want, no matter how big or small IT may be. These three simple steps can be a catalyst for major change if you understand each on its own and all three together as a strategy. The end goal here is for you to be able to do the following, on command, regardless of the challenges you may face.

1. Think about what you really want (not just what you think you can get).

2. Invest focus and energy in that direction (get the ball rolling).

3. Eliminate the limiting beliefs in your way (a.k.a., shut Betty up).

4. Ingrain new empowering beliefs as a foundation (build some internal strength).

5. Start taking action in the right direction to get the results you want.

Walt Disney said, "If you can dream it, you can do it."

Everyone dreams. But most people stop when they wake up. Why?

The same four reasons I believe we develop stories which become limiting beliefs...

1. Keep us SAFE from failure or pain

2. Feed the EGO to cover up the pain and feel significant

3. Keep us in conformity with others so we feel ACCEPTED

4. JUSTIFY why it is this way so we don't have to change, we have certainty

Any of these starting to hit home yet?

Well what If I were to tell you the world was flat at one point?

And we would never be able to fly? Or women will never be allowed to vote? I'd be wrong on all three counts and yet people would have been willing to die for these beliefs at some point in time. But, more importantly, someone dreamed of things being different.

Someone envisioned something greater, something to expand our consciousness, believed they could achieve it and went to work to make it so.

In order for the world to be what it is today, millions of dreamers had to go out on a limb and think differently. Many of whom we celebrate for their out-of-the-box thinking, long after the fact.

I have always envisioned myself inspiring other women as I have been influenced by many inspiring female mentors myself whether I knew them personally or not. What better way to carry the torch and continue the legacy of women encouraging women than to do the same for others. I found a deep passion to pave the way, instead of follow it. And wanted to inspire others to do the same not by my words, but by my action.

I have been fortunate to do so by leading large retail organizations across Canada, the United States, and Australia. I fell in love with helping young women become aware of their potential and guiding them to build belief in themselves, take massive action, and get results.

What I envisioned came fully to fruition two years ago when, coincidentally, I was introduced to two women who shared my vision for an organization of women empowering women. It was a mutual connection who happened to have a similar conversation with all three of us and called it to our attention, suggesting we explore it. Sometimes we all need a little nudge from someone on the outside who can see it a little more clearly than we can.

It was this one small connection that led to a conversation that led to a meeting. A series of these meetings then took place with the three of us together brainstorming and sharing our passion for change — ultimately leading to an international movement inspiring thousands of women around the world to go after what they want in life and support each other in the process.

That dream came true. In a matter of months, something we were so driven to see come alive, with a bit of hard work and commitment, happened. And it became one big beautiful family of inspiring women all working together to motivate and encourage each other.

When you are able to accomplish something that at one time you thought impossible, you start to wonder what else you can accomplish. Suddenly the possibilities are endless.

None of that would have happened if I had simply thought it as a wish or a nice thought. It took planning, a lot of action, some being uncomfortable, and a bunch of failing. But it was all worth it; I would do it again a hundred times over. It was with this organization that I truly began to understand what living your purpose means and the impact it can have on those around you and the world at large.

What started as an idea, a dream, became a question of What if? Not what if we did do it, but what if we didn't?

When you yourself are inspired to change, everyone around you cannot help but notice and think a little differently than they did before.

Where did I start? I had to envision what I wanted. I had to put aside all the reasons why I couldn't or why it wouldn't work and simply dream, dream big.

"The future belongs to those who believe in the beauty of their dreams."
—Eleanor Roosevelt

…And to those who turn the page and start PART 3 now!

Part Three:
GET A LIFE!
(THE ONE YOU ACTUALLY WANT)

CHAPTER NINETEEN

Belief is the New Black

19

Envision

---

*"**W**ithout leaps of imagination, or dreaming,
we lose the excitement of possibilities. Dreaming,
after all, is a form of planning."*
—*Gloria Steinem*

---

1. GET REAL

By 'get real' I don't mean realistic. I mean it's time to get real with yourself! Get naked! What do you want? What do you really, really, really want? Be honest; don't deny yourself the pleasure of a dream. Put aside all the fears and the reasons why it can't happen. Just let it go and let it flow. Give yourself some quiet alone time to sit with a pen and paper in a comfortable place with no distractions and think about the following questions.

What do I want my life to look like?

What am I passionate about?

What do I love doing?

What do I want to accomplish?

Write each question in the middle of a piece of paper inside a bubble. Each answer is then an offshoot with another bubble. You want to create a mind map of all the possibilities! Mind maps work like our creative mind works, expanding in every direction. Take as much time as you need and don't stop until you have exhausted yourself and you have IDEAS inside bubbles all over the place.

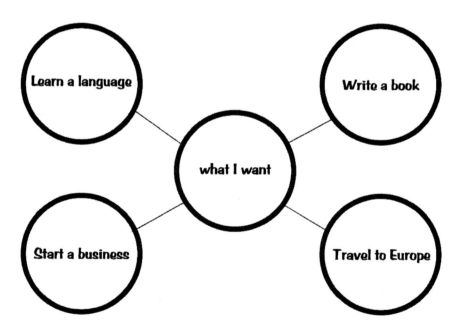

This is just an example, don't limit yourself, draw as many bubbles as you want!

The questions you are answering are a mix of what you want, and what you love or are passionate about. Answering these unabashedly, wholeheartedly, and just for you can lead you to the burning desire, the thing you would go to war for, something that gets you out of bed and into your belief cape every day, do or die. It just might be hidden behind the same veil of fear I had.

You might already know what you want, in which case this exercise could be an opportunity to expand and get specific. Or maybe this activity will uncover a whole new area of excitement. You'll start to see common themes show up, maybe even things you knew you wanted but were too afraid to admit in the past for fear of inadequacy or failure. Or you didn't see how you could obtain something you desired so you didn't allow yourself to think it was even possible. Whatever it is be excited about it. Most people don't think about what they really want; they only allow themselves to think as far as what they think they can get. They stay inside the comfort zone. So give yourself this gift and enjoy this time of beautiful self-exploration.

Now, circle or highlight the ideas or themes that show up multiple times. For example, is it starting your own business? Is it teaching others a skill or helping people? Is it traveling the world or like me- writing a book?

Whatever (whoever or wherever) those desires are, write each one separately on a new piece of paper for each. If you have two desires, then you should have two pieces of paper.

(Think, Marnie Kay, 2013 The Year of the Entrepreneur!)

2. PICTURE IT

Mind map round 2. This time, with the desire in mind close your eyes, envision that you have already accomplished it and ask yourself...

What specifically do I need to see, hear, feel, touch, and smell or taste (if applicable) in order to know for sure that I have it?

What specifically needs to happen in order for me to know that I have achieved this?

For example, what I needed to see in order to know that I had accomplished my goal of inspiring women to pursue their passions was messages and stories from those I had impacted, a growing organization and new opportunities everyday to share the message of women empowering women coming to us. All of which I was clearly able to identify when it happened.

We think in pictures so the whole point of this exercise is to get a really clear picture in your mind of what success looks like to you. This should be an exciting, fun, and inspiring activity. It's one you can revisit every so often as you accomplish your goals and a new level of possibility begins to expand your world even more.

It was through doing this activity years ago that I even realized what I was passionate about. I thought I was living my passion but the truth was far from it. In taking the time to really think about what I wanted, regardless of the money or time I would need to accomplish it, I had a really clear image in my mind that I could envision, live and practice in my mind. I knew exactly what I was going for, even if I didn't know how I would get it. I could see it.

One of the most influential and celebrated self-help leaders of this century, Jim Rohn has said "The bigger the why, the easier the how." When you want something badly enough, you will find a way.

3. WRITE IT DOWN, EVERYWHERE.

It's not enough to occasionally think about what you want— this merely constitutes a wish. And we know where wishing gets us… (You're on the plane to Hawaii for a fabulous vacation and you've actually gained weight instead of getting rid of the fifteen pounds you wished to lose.)

Wishes are for wimps. We are not wimps.

This part of the process is to write down what you want, as if you have already achieved it—positive and in the future with an identifiable feeling attached. It's one thing to think that owning your own business would be nice, it's another to know that you will feel driven to succeed and completely motivated to make a difference when you own your own (insert passion here) business with a support team of five of the best, and your role is the leader and visionary for future growth. See the difference?

Get out a pen, paper, sticky notes, your cell phone, your computer desktop, diaries and journals, notebooks and pocketbooks, a blank wall in your home and the mirror in your bathroom. Everything that you come across in a day should have this written in it or on it somewhere for you to remind yourself and read aloud.

Many successful people have taught this simple task as a way to keep you on track to reaching your goals. I truly believe it was this activity that I fully committed to, that kept me focused on where I wanted to go, instead of where I was. It helped me build the vision in my mind to be strong, clear and a constant motivator.

Were you ever told in class stop daydreaming? Well, we are bringing it back in style!

For example:

"I am so confident and empowered now that I am toned, fit, healthy and full of vibrant energy to do more."

Attach a date by when you want this accomplished. It must be a date you believe you could achieve, even if it might be a stretch for you. Now every time you read this you must be able to visualize the picture you have of yourself accomplishing it. The key is to really be able to feel the accomplishment and live the moment in your mind. Notice how you feel when you have that clear picture in your mind?

You're not done yet!

Write this down everywhere. Everywhere you visit often, such as the bathroom, your office, a desk, or a side table. Give yourself a good five to ten locations that you visit frequently, throughout the day forcing yourself to visualize the accomplishment in your mind. Build that dream, baby! It starts with a picture in your mind.

4. MAKE IT STICK

We believe in things we can't see all the time. This is the key to magic.

"You have to imagine it possible before you can see something. You can have it right in front of you, but if you can't imagine something that has never existed before, it's impossible."
—Rita Dove

Writing it down and visualizing it is what gives you the story that it can and will happen, but what usually happens along the way after we set a big scary goal?

Let me answer this with a question. Ever seen a gym in January? It's packed to the rim. People are waiting for machines and trying to do the exercise classes all squished in the corner. It's a mess. Mayhem. Everyone is just trying to get in shape after an unnecessarily indulgent happy holidays.

Let's fast forward to February. Same gym, same time of day. It's completely empty. All of the happy January gym-goers are suddenly paying rent for something they won't likely use again until the following January. Great revenue stream of residual income for gym owners, but unfortunately, it's truly a lost cause for anyone who can't stick to a goal for longer than three weeks.

We know that pain is a stronger motivation than pleasure; this, coupled with a fading vision of what you want, equals a quick trip down the [8]slippery dip of giving up.

The real reason a gym looks like a zombie apocalypse actually happened is that the vision wasn't strong enough for most of the gym-goers. Either they were focused on what they didn't want (i.e. the weight they were trying to lose) or the image of what they wanted wasn't a burning desire or a must have. How do they get it in that category?

---

8 "Slippery dip" is Australian for "slippery slide."

Focus on and visualize what you want relentlessly.

So, while you are reading your written affirmations all over the place, you need to hold a strong image of what it looks like in your mind. Find pictures online, in books or magazines, of what you want, what success looks like for that desire, and pin it up on a vision board or somewhere highly visible in your home where you can remind yourself what it looks like until that image is strong in your mind.

This is very powerful. And many of us probably have examples of times when we have done this unconsciously. I have many times. One example I can think of was when I was about nine years old, I had a fascination with polar bears. I don't know why. I lived in Australia, far from where polar bears could exist comfortably. I didn't care where in the world they lived, I loved them. One day I found a picture of a polar bear in a store, it was three images of the same polar bear in a spread.

After I haggled the sales lady to drop the price (I started negotiating at a young age) this picture hung above my bed in my bedroom in my parent's home until the day I moved to Canada. I didn't even know polar bears were in Canada but when I found out where Canada was, I connected the dots. I get that polar bears are not a significant goal to be accomplished as such, but you can see the correlation of how I visualized something every day, and I here

I am. Voilà!

In all seriousness, anything you have accomplished in life was at first a thought in your mind, a belief that it could happen, followed by the actions you took to get there.

In a world where we constantly quit things when they get too hard, or seem impossible, the winners are the ones who don't quit, the ones who hold the vision, despite all apparent odds.

All of this is simply the power of suggestion. Not a new concept. The power of suggestion is constantly employed by all mainstream marketing today to get us to think what they want us to think and more importantly buy. We oblige, often unknowingly. Ever called a tissue a 'kleenex'? The power of suggestion is powerful no matter what the suggestion.

Therefore, suggesting to yourself that it is possible and, in fact, already done in your mind is critical. We've established that our beliefs often begin with an idea, a story that we tell ourselves- sometimes merely a suggestion. For better or worse. You are the gatekeeper.

"Not fulfilling your dreams will be a loss to the world, because the world needs everyone's gift-yours and mine."
—Barbara Sher

CHAPTER TWENTY

Belief is the New Black

20

Ingrain

"Success is often achieved by those who do not know that failure is inevitable"

—Coco Chanel

Once you've decided what you want the fear sets in, along with the questions and the doubt. Can I? Do I know how? You come up with all the reasons it won't work. Betty is back. It's familiar and just feels so much easier to gradually, then suddenly give up. I just have one question…

How is that working for you? Giving up?

Or maybe you're just lacking in the belief that it will happen. It's unchartered territory, out of the comfort zone, you haven't walked the mile yet and, therefore, you don't know what it looks like. That was a good story before you knew better, but now we need to eliminate the limiting beliefs stopping you from moving forward and INGRAIN the empowering ones.

Step 1: IDENTIFY the limiting beliefs holding you back

"Believe. No pessimist ever discovered the secrets of the stars, or sailed to unchartered land, or opened a new heaven to the human spirit."
—Helen Keller

The first step is identifying or uncovering where you may be limiting yourself with your beliefs. This requires you to be completely honest with yourself (naked remember?) and completely open and willing to address what might be deeply hidden behind that veil.

So how do you find out if you have a limiting belief? Simple. Take a look at your life and find an area that is unsatisfactory to you or even just not where you want it to be. It could be finances, career, health, or relationships.

Now ask yourself the following questions. Again, work with the mind map technique so your mind can be completely free to wander instead of constrained to a list. Then ask yourself the following questions while drawing bubbles with your challenges and branching out to go as deep as you can!

What area of my life has less than satisfactory results right now?

What (within this area) am I not doing, that I know I need to do?

What specifically (within this area) am I not good at?

What specifically could I improve to get better results?

What is the hardest thing to do?

What do I like doing the least?

Now for all the challenges listed on the page, write out a why for each one.

WHY am I not doing what I know I need to do?

WHY am I not good at these areas?

WHY is this hard for me to do?

WHY don't I like doing this?

This should uncover a nice list of some juicy limiting beliefs (that, for the most part, aren't true) we can work on getting rid of next. But, before that, we are going to take this one step further. In order to move away from the pain and toward the pleasure, we need to really understand the impact, the pain you aren't actually aware of by holding onto the limiting belief. Remember that pain, somewhere down the road, will reveal its full impact—gradually then suddenly.

Let's check the damage here by answering these questions for yourself...

1) What is the price I have paid as a result of believing this?

2) How is this belief affecting me emotionally, physically, mentally, and financially?

3) What would be the benefit of getting rid of this limiting belief?

All right, are you in it? Feeling all gross and honest? Great, let's keep it moving.

Step 2: Belief Blowout

"We cannot direct the wind but we can adjust the sails."
—Dolly Parton

It's important to note here just how far you have come. Think of all the progress you have made thus far. First, you learned to understand how our beliefs work, then how you can change them and make better decisions.

Once you've identified some of the limiting beliefs holding

you back (and you've probably just now seen how many you might be harboring), it's time to blow it up and show yourself it's simply a story you are telling yourself.

What if it's not true?
What if you or someone else made it up, and what if you could get rid of it with just a few key questions?

I deviate for a minute and take this back to a time in my life when I was broke. I literally poured wine back into the bottle to save some, lived on canned tuna and Subway sandwiches. I was broke. I had massive debt on multiple credit cards and no sign of improvement. The crazy part was I was earning a six-figure income. Something was wrong. And when something is as obviously wrong as this, it all ties back to the limiting beliefs we have and the strategies we carry out to confirm these beliefs in our mind. Then they materialize into results in front of you. To show you what I mean by this, here is an example of an exact conversation I had with myself regularly at that time in my life.

"How am I going to get out of this mess? I feel like it's just getting worse and worse. I wish someone would help me, but I'm so broke no one would even lend me money at this point. I get paid next week, and I should probably put some money away then. So, if I'm going to do that I might as well at least have a good time this week and go out and just spend! It'll make me feel better and, besides, I deserve it. I've worked really hard this week."

I was running this story, this strategy for everything in my life. Thinking that happiness was the result instead of the inspiration.

This story is what landed me in a seemingly unsalvageable financial situation. Not to mention an emotional rollercoaster with exhilarating highs and destructive lows. It was almost like some sort of legal drug that I had developed a strategy to live with. While I had been diagnosed with depression and anxiety, for years I shoveled the pain and confusion under a pile of shopping, credit card debt, and the purchasing of unnecessary extravagances, thinking all of it would make me feel better.

I really believed I wasn't in charge of my life. It was happening to me and I had no way of making a decision to be happy unless something changed for me. What snapped me out of this horrible self-talk loop of doom? Well, it was one dramatic emotional event, and the decision I made to change.

When something as dramatic as the loss of a loved one, or an accident or a major change takes place in your life, you are left to pick up pieces and put everything back together, but it doesn't fit the way it used to. What you believed before now has a big hole in it.

So I could start to question other beliefs I carried behind me in my expensive portable luggage. Prior to my mum's death, I lived in a world where nothing really serious could ever happen. I lived in space where avoidance ruled, I had plenty of time to fix things or say what I want to say later. Then… Bam! Those beliefs were shattered in a million little pieces and I was left completely open to possibility with the chance to learn and grow as so much of what I thought I knew was no longer true.

The entire reason for this book, this message, and my stories is to show you it doesn't have to take a dramatic emotional event to change your perspective. You can get rid of those limiting beliefs and begin living life the way you want right now. But it might take a cold slap in the face to wake you up. That's what I'm here for. I promise I won't even enjoy it a little bit. The only problem is that this cold slap must be repeated. The same way you ingrained all the limiting beliefs in your world is the same way you get rid of them. There is no easy way out of change.

Repetition of a new idea, an empowering belief, can change everything; in fact, it's how you developed the beliefs you have in the first place.

Once you've found a limiting belief, ask yourself… For what purpose am I choosing to hold onto this belief?

Is it Ego? Protection? Is it so you can fit in? Is it out of fear?

The purpose of the belief I was holding onto was simple. It protected me. I was afraid. If I finally made the decision, if I could do something to change it all, I wouldn't know where to start. I might fail. Oh, hey, Betty. As long as I reinforced the beliefs I held, I sabotaged myself by spending money to feel good and just landed even further in debt. I was safe with my secure job so that would have to do. The debt kept me in the job and the job kept me in debt. That's a vicious circle right there, one in which so many people are stuck.

It wasn't until I had had enough of accepting what was given to me and finally admitted that I wanted things to change that I realized I had to change them. No one else. This one was on me. So I started writing it down, repeating it aloud to myself until my beliefs changed. The limiting ones started to seem smaller and insignificant and the empowering ones just got bigger and stronger. I started to feel like things were possible and that I could find a way.

Believe me, this is not a one-hit wonder. This is like Celine Dion's career. You have to sing the same damn song over and over again until you believe.

Another way to look at these limiting beliefs is understanding where they might have come from? What was the ignition or the source? Try asking yourself these questions…

Where was I when I decided to believe this?

What was the last event before I decided to believe this?

This will help you understand your strategy in building a belief and answer the following questions so you can more easily identify where it starts for you and how to stop it.

What leads to my beliefs?

What has to happen in order for me to believe something?

Is it someone credible to me?

Is it something I see?

What types of proof do I look for to believe something?

Keep going. Show yourself that your beliefs are made up. Interrogate yourself and don't let yourself off the hook easily. Your life depends on it!

Am I as sure of this as the sun will come up tomorrow?

Have I been wrong in something I believed before?

Could this be false? If so, what might suggest that this is false?

What else could this mean?

You should by now have a big question mark on what you believe about yourself. If not just yet, you might be at least questioning the idea a little. This is good. This is the beginning. Now to get some good stuff in there instead.

Step 3: Ingrain empowering beliefs

Ingraining empowering beliefs is simply replacing the ones that don't work for you with ones that do work for you, the same way you created the ones that aren't working for you.

TELL THE STORY THAT FEELS GOOD OVER AND OVER AND OVER AGAIN.

The first real relationship destroyer for my mum and I came about when I was fourteen. My mum had started dating another man, the first after my dad, and I was probably likely harboring some resentment on the issue. I was trying to get on with my bad self in my teenage years at high school. A wonderful, fiery combination of a shit-uation. So I had decided to start testing the limits, as teenagers often do. I was skipping class, telling the teachers their class was a waste of time—things of that sort. And there came a point when I believed I had probably done a bit too much damage at my current school by the ninth grade. Questions were being asked of me that I didn't like, and it was time to get the heck out of dodge. Plus, my crazy off-the-wall best friend at the time had convinced me another school would have fewer rules and we could make some new friends that would better understand us. With that convincing argument, I was in. I was ready for a new school, new friends, and an opportunity to run away from a bit of a mess I had stirred up. Little did I know at the time this would become a theme in my life.

The decision wasn't going to be the hard part. Telling—or asking—my parents would be. I started with my dad which went surprisingly well; he wasn't concerned. He applauded my decision for a school that might grade me tougher (this was my reasoning for wanting to switch schools) and supported my decision wholeheartedly. Phew! I assumed my conversation with my mother would go similarly, but it turns out I severely overestimated my persuasion abilities after the smooth agreement with my dad.

It couldn't have gone worse. Over the phone we erupted into an explosive discussion with what I could see as no real argument on her end. She played the mother card: she makes the decisions when it comes to school. Pffft. This didn't resonate with me; I could just live with dad since he agreed with me. And so I did. As of that day, she told me, "If you make this decision and go against me, you are not welcome in my home." This I did agree on; I told her it was my decision. I hung up. Good-bye. Angry teenage foot stomp.

This was the beginning of the end of the relationship I had with my mother. For six months I avoided conversations. My dad would tell me, "You'll have to talk to her at some point; she is your mother." But I was angry, hurt, and felt entitled. I had developed this story over time where she was easily the worst mother on earth and she would be lucky to have me back. Even writing that sounds awful but it was the truth; that was how I felt.

Over time we rekindled our relationship somewhat and worked hard to regain some of the trust that was broken. We licked our wounds and agreed to disagree, or disregard the entire thing. We buried the hatchet deep down.

Our relationship consisted of a perpetual cycle of letdown, problem, repair, letdown, problem, repair. At least that's the story I told myself to keep my expectations low so I couldn't be hurt again, too much. The day my sister called to tell me she had died, all of this seemed to flood through me. I was full of blame and anger one last time because she had left me before we could fix it. I kept running the same stories to try and make sense of it all and move on, but the truth was I had to learn to forgive myself, not her.

The stories I kept replaying would be on repeat as long as I couldn't forgive myself for the decisions I had made, the hurt I had caused, and the blame and guilt I had felt. It was all a choice in the first place, and now I had the same choice to make. I had to forgive myself; I had to start to tell a story that just felt better.

Tell a better story. Tell the story that feels good.

Do you have anything you've hung onto? A story or a belief? Something that you know deep down affects your relationships, trust, and love even now, long after the experience? Now imagine finding a diary of the person involved, where he or she had written his or her thoughts and feelings at the time—another side of the same story yet completely different. I did. After my mum died, I went through everything furiously looking for answers and a connection, anything to feel close or to try and understand. It was an old address book that I found (God knows why she wrote it in the back of an address book), dated back to 1995. It was written in her distinct handwriting, her version of the story that now for me seemed a little hazy and unclear.

Reading her version started to blur mine and made me question the story I had developed and the truth in it all. Who was right? Which story was real? The blurry emotional one in my mind, or the in-the-moment version captured by her, on paper in front of me?

The answer is both. Both were right. And that's why neither of us were happy with our relationship. I've heard many times that 'you can be right or you can be happy'. I needed to be right for so long, that I gave up being happy in the process. I'm going to go out on a limb and suggest I got my stubbornness from her. We hung so tightly to our beliefs and our story that the other couldn't possibly be true. And yet there it was right in front of me as if she had gotten the last word in. At first I was mad that I couldn't argue it with her, so I decided to ask my brother and sister for their versions of the story. My brother didn't really remember and my sister pieced together some simple version of it like, "I don't know; didn't you just decide to live with Dad for a while when you changed schools?"

You can be right or you can be happy.

It was with this realization I was able to comprehend how unbelievably creative we can be, how masterful in storytelling we can become, in order to support and reinforce what we need to be true.

Knowing now that it's all a beautiful creation—the good, the bad, and the ugly—then it's up to us to create the good ones. How do we do that? Well, the same way we create the ugly ones.

It is easier to convince yourself of something than someone else.

REPETITION

Gina Mollicone-Long, the teacher I mentioned earlier (and who so graciously wrote the foreword to this book), once told me to take a few minutes every morning and every night to look myself in the eyes in the mirror. Take a few deep breaths and tell myself 'I love you' a bunch of times. "See what happens," she said, as she grinned cunningly. She's not one for mucking around, so I knew there was something in it for me. She also isn't one for giving the answer, so I also knew I would have to figure it out along the way.

The whole experiment started out ridiculous. First of all, I couldn't take myself seriously. Second, I couldn't say it out loud because someone might hear me. So I halfheartedly put myself in the position every day to carry out her instructions. It's funny, though: what started out with me inspecting my teeth for a possible floss move, whispering 'I love you' while I tugged the skin on my face backward to see what a facelift might look like, today has more depth and emotion than I could have ever imagined.

This moment actually became a beautiful soulful meditation with myself every day. Slowly I began to take it seriously. I went from inside my head, to whispers, to saying it aloud. Before I knew it, as if all of a sudden, I felt it. I could feel the love for myself growing as I had truly begun to believe what I had been suggesting. I went from giggling at myself to giggling with myself in joy, feeling beautiful and inspired by the feeling I could create just with three simple words and a little eyeball stare-down. I decided I didn't need a facelift.

The power of suggestion is a simple repetitive action that can change your mood, your state, and your mind. As a result, it is has carried religions, wars, corporations, and governments for longer than we know.

The repetition of an idea or suggestion can plant thoughts that become ideas, which then become the stories we tell ourselves and ultimately what we believe. Before you know it, it's as if it were always there.

So let's use this power we have for good! Find one of those ugly beliefs. Have a look at something you identified in the previous exercises, a belief or a story that's holding you back. And work through the following...

TRY THIS ON:

What would you have to believe in order for this to not be true?

For example:

Who am I to think I could write a book that people would want to read?

Q. What would I have to believe in order for this to not be true?

A. I would have to believe that I have much to offer in a book that others would enjoy reading and similarly be inspired to pursue a passion.

Now close your eyes and visualize...

What would have to happen for you to know you have been successful?

What would it look like if this were to happen?

Where would you be?

Who would be there with you?

What would be happening around you?

What would you hear, see, smell, taste, feel?

How much better does that feel? Do you feel inspired to take action now?

When we can suggest a better story and play the part (e.g., I am a sought after speaker and author, and my book has impacted millions of women and girls) you can change how you feel. When you can change how you feel, you can change your beliefs and start to take inspired action toward your goals.

So it is simple. Create an empowering belief. Ingrain it deep inside by repeating it to yourself out loud, really feel the emotion of it's achievement as if you already have achieved it. Pretend you believe it until you do. And you will.

"Believe that life is worth living and your belief will help create the fact."
—William James

CHAPTER TWENTY-ONE
Belief is the New Black

21

Engage

"The most effective way to do it, is to do it."
—Amelia Earhart

Most people don't set goals. Of those who do, most quit before they even start. In my opinion, there are a few simple yet dramatic differences between those who achieve success and those who don't.

For starters, successful people start. They launch, take action, and move forward in the direction of their dreams.

It sounds simple enough, however, this is often the barrier for most. The thought or dream is full of doubt and all the stories of why it won't work and might be too hard—or even impossible—start to creep in. Therefore, those who start (inspite of the same fears we all have) are already a monstrous step ahead of everyone else.

The second difference I have come to notice is perseverance.

Those who don't quit surely achieve more than those who do by default. When some of the most successful people are interviewed, it's often stories of failure, heartache, and struggle. And yet here they are in all their shining armor looking, as if they just floated their way to the top. This is probably the single biggest reason most don't even start. We don't see all of the struggles, financial difficulties, or failures behind the scenes as someone builds his or her dreams. We only see the finished result and think, well, obviously they got lucky! I could never do that.

The self-help industry is a genius industry worth trillions of dollars. Why? Humans quit. We quit jobs, relationships, friendships, diets, and gym memberships. We quit sometimes before we even start.

Perseverance or self-discipline is something we have to develop. It's quite often the difference-maker. In order to get what we want, we have to become the person who will do the work through self-discipline when others will not.

I'll use the example of J. K. Rowling, the first self-made billionaire author in history. After much turmoil in a failed marriage, the death of her mother, and living on welfare, she went to work every day building what she felt compelled to do when most others would give up. She went on to be rejected by twelve publishers and, finally, the thirteenth one took on her project, not without a warning from her agent suggesting she would never make money writing children's books. Thankfully, she ignored that.

At the Harvard commencement speech in 2008, J. K. Rowling graciously shared her lessons in life. **Failure**, she referred to as being absolutely necessary, and **imagination** integral to a life having been worth lived. Of the entire speech, the following was for me the most profound, coming from a rags-to-riches life built from a single dream to write…

I was set free, because my greatest fear had been realized, and I was still alive. Rock bottom became the solid foundation on which I built my life.

You might never fail on the scale I did. But some failure in life is inevitable, it is impossible to live without failing at something, unless you live so cautiously that you might not have lived at all. In which case you fail by default.

Failure is the gateway to success. I will repeat that: failure is the gateway to success. It is through failure that we learn and grow and become who we need to become in order to achieve what we want to achieve. And we can only reach the gateway of failure by starting and persevering.

Starting and persevering are intrinsically entwined. I'll use this book as an example. It all began somewhere back in time a few years ago. I started writing creatively again and wanted to wrap it all into a book. At my request, a few friends who had some experience in the industry of media read my book with criticism. They both decided it needed a lot of work and so I gave up. I Quit. Too hard! I'm probably not a great writer; these book reviewers would know better. Though maybe I'll pick it up again in a few years when I have more time to perfect my creative writing craft.

Sure enough a year later I took another crack at it. Ultimately, I loved the creative feel of pouring my mind out into words for others to read, yet I was so completely terrified someone might not like it or suggest it "needs a lot of work." Why I rested so heavily on other's opinions of my creativity I'll never know. But as sure as the sun came up I quit... again. It's not going the way I want, and I just don't have the kind of time I need to apply right now. See how this goes?

So here it is another year later and I'm on the verge of completion (or as you are reading this, obviously a finished product). So what's the difference? What changed?

I haven't just sat down to write. I have searched deep into the idea—the what, the why, and the who. I asked myself some of the tough questions to build the burning desire to have a finished product and a result I am proud of. I have a clear vision of where I am going and what the purpose is for me and everyone else. I know what I want.

I ingrained the empowering belief that I can, that I have value to give. If others can learn from my experiences, then what an amazing gift I give to the world. I believe I am worthy and capable.

I am engaging in the activities required for accomplishment. I am Do-ing. I'm taking action. I have set deadlines to hold myself accountable and found those around me who can support me with peer accountability to help guide the creative process. They don't read and criticize with their creative viewpoint but provide valuable input that I decide to take and learn from or file away for later.

Honestly, anything successful in my life was done with these three steps: 1) I decided what I wanted (ENVISION), 2) I replaced a limiting belief with an empowering belief that I could have it (INGRAIN), and 3) I took the gloves off, got out there, and did something about it (ENGAGE).

Success or results in anything isn't a sudden arrival. It's highly likely that it won't be any one major thing that is going to change your entire life but, instead, an accumulation of all the small things done well.

The reason I was offered the role of overseeing the entire

state for the music retailer at age nineteen, or when I was hired to oversee eastern Canada and the United States for a department in which I had no formal training, wasn't because I suddenly knew everything or achieved the sales plan a few times. It was my ability to persevere in everything I did, day in and day out. It was the little things that I consistently finished, the leaders I developed over time through daily conversations. Although they often seemed small in the moment, I never underestimated their worth in the long run. Things happened gradually then suddenly.

So it is here that I leave you some tips on taking action. I promise if you commit to engage each of these five ideas or empowering beliefs, you will see progress. And, if you persist, you will see results.

LIGHTS, CAMERA, ACTION!

First in, best dressed.

If this doesn't get you moving, I don't know what will. We are in a world where everyone is in competition for jobs, for people, for the best sales on Black Friday at Macy's. You need not look at everything like a competition, but know this: if you don't do it, someone else will. Who would you rather get the contract, the sale, or the role? You. So what are you going to do about it to set yourself apart? Whatever you do, do it now.

In Olympic swimming, often the first swimmer off the block has a massive advantage, a few seconds ahead of the dive. His or her confidence increases and the likelihood of a better swim is high. Whether you're diving off a block or getting started on an idea, your initial success is all related to your reaction time. Reaction time is the time it takes from the spark, the thought, or the idea to surface and you to get moving. A slow reaction time is often the result of the stories we are busy telling ourselves combined with some procrastination or laziness. While the losers are criticizing the others' choices in swimwear, the winners are already off the block.

What is your reaction time? Do you often see women wearing something and think, I was going to get one of those? Do you ever see someone create a program or a business and think, I thought of doing that a while ago? If you have ever had this thought before, your reaction time is slow, to say the least. Time to boost that baby up. From now on, write down every idea you have—no matter how silly or unrealistic it may seem. Then give yourself five minutes to explore it at some point in that day; use the mind map. What are the possibilities? Could it lead somewhere? What resources do you have now to put the idea in motion? Watch that reaction time diminish as you begin to explore the possibility instead of accepting the impossibility. Find ways you can take action now.

Do the thing you don't want to do first.

Of all the tips I have learned about taking action, this is the hardest to commit to. No one wants to do the things they don't want to do. However, sometimes this is the thing that could be the key to a breakthrough. It's often when we do the things that we thought we couldn't do, that a whole world of new possibilities open up. You have now stepped out of that boring old comfort zone and made the other tasks ahead of you seem insignificant and probably easy.

"You gain strength, courage, and confidence by every experience in which you really stop to look fear in the face. You are able to say to yourself, 'I lived through this horror. I can take the next thing that comes along.' You must do the thing you think you cannot do."
—Eleanor Roosevelt

So begin every day with this in mind. Write down that one big task, the one thing that scares you that you know will drive you forward, whether it be personally in relationships or in business. Hold yourself accountable to completing it. If you need help (and you know your self-accountability needs help) then tell someone what you plan to do and why. Have them suggest a reward when completed. Now, not only do you have someone waiting on you to do it, you also have an incentive. Who doesn't love an incentive?

First things first. Do things in the order they need to be done not the order of comfort level. Change that up and watch your results change too.

Act as if

Begin with the end in mind. Once you know where you are going, asusme the role, become the example of what or who you wish to be, do or have or give. Find those around you who have what you want and model their behavior.

When Oprah started out in television, she modeled herself after Barbara Walters.

She defined Barbara as success, Barbara had what she wanted. So Oprah studied Barbara. She would sit like her, talk like her, and emulate her every move until she no longer needed a source for what success looked like. Oprah herself had become success.

Act as if. While in university, I landed the lead role in a Brisbane City production of Much Ado about Nothing, a Shakespeare play that was to run for almost eight weeks straight, I actually didn't intend to audition. There was no possible way I could fit it in to my already busy student schedule at the age of eighteen. However, a friend at the time was auditioning for the lead role and encouraged me to go along with her and audition so she wouldn't be alone.

I reluctantly agreed. With no time to prepare a memorized part I grabbed a particularly emotional monologue of Desdemona from one of the more tragic Shakespeare plays, Othello. I figured I would have some fun with it and go big before I went home. In this scene Desdemona pleads with the main character's friend to go and beg for forgiveness of her husband who believes she has cheated on him, which is untrue. The verse itself is quite heart wrenching and portrays the "damsel in distress"—incidentally the exact character they wanted for the lead in the play they were casting. My friend decided to do a monologue of a Shakespearian man, probably not what they were going for, and she might have chosen to do a little more thinking on the appropriateness of monologue choice. (Extra tip: take the right action)

Anyway, I nervously threw myself on the stage and, with my script in hand, went for it wholeheartedly as if I already had the lead role. I cried, I beat the floor as I knelt down in anguish, feeling every ounce of the emotional pain of Desdemona I could find within me.

What felt like five seconds was actually about five minutes of weeping and wailing. I finally opened my eyes to check on the director's reaction; there was a big cheesy grin on his face.

I left for the day with my unenthusiastic friend. She spent the afternoon assuring me she had landed the role despite my "over-the-top audition," as she referred to it. Not even a few hours later the director called to let me know he had cast me as the lead and how impressed he was with my audition. I got it. I was quite impressed with myself. My friend however, was not...

Sure this is acting, so 'act as if' makes sense in this regard.

However, I have continued to apply this attitude in everything I do. When you take on the role or the position or the attitude you need to portray, vocally, physically, and emotionally, you put yourself in a state of readiness where the mind can believe or take on whatever is in front of you.

This is how I was promoted to the position of area manager by the age of 19, running a $100MM business by the age of 26 and managed an entire department (for which I had no formal education or training) for Eastern Canada and the United States of America. None of which I knew how to do before I did it.

In whatever you are aiming to do, think of what success looks like and do that, become that.

Be BOLD!

This doesn't mean be loud and obnoxious. It means be decisive, dare to do what everyone else won't. Look for what others avoid and get out there and do it. Being bold means going where no one else has gone or is willing to go; it's often the most successful people who simply dared to do what others would not.

"Don't be intimidated by what you don't know. That can be your greatest strength and ensure that you do things differently from everyone else."
—Sara Blakely

Many a successful person has built an empire from something others deemed undesirable. Let's take Sara Blakely, founder of the line of undergarment body-tightening SPANX and the world's youngest self-made female billionaire. She is definitely someone worth paying attention to.

Now let's break this down for a second. Ten years ago no one would have spoken of the underwear they wore for an evening to suck everything in, even if they wouldn't go anywhere without it. One woman, single handedly, boldly, created an unbeatable version (nothing ultimately new, just better) and marketed it in a way that almost made it sexy? Now women wear and talk about their SPANX like it's a new shade of lipstick that enhances your pout, instead of a skin-coloured pair of really tight underwear.

Sara Blakely took something fairly undesirable, developed the 'Apple' of the undergarment industry, and put it in your face. And she became one of the richest self-made women in the history of female entrepreneurs. Underwear. Enough said. It pays to be bold—

billions of dollars, in fact.

But being Bold isn't about being rude, nasty or down right annoying. Being bold happens on the inside. It is often making a tough decision through failures or believing in something when no one else does. Bob Proctor, who I have previously referenced and followed closely for the last ten years of my life, has said, "Fear and faith both require you to believe in something you cannot see. You choose."

Being BOLD is choosing faith because most people choose fear. The world today is governed by fear. Almost every decision we make comes from a place of fear, of pain and suffering, loss, hurt, anger, or being alone.

So, do the opposite; choose faith and ingrain the empowering belief of possibility. It's amazing what this one small shift can do for your entire life. And it is simply a choice, a decision to desire something different and to be willing to work for it.

But this is the trick! In order to begin making effective decisions and see the possibility, the potential and that it's really all YOU, you need to become the person you need to be in order to be successful. Often we think, when I get money, then I can finally be happy, excited, motivated etc.

But this is backward. In order to have money and success, you need to be happy, excited, motivated and hardworking already. Think about your days when you wake up in bad mood. How does

does the rest of your day look? How you show up is representative of what you'll get in life. How we do anything means everything. Be bold.

Find a PURPOSE

A large part of having the energy to spring into action and be inspired to do what you need to do is about feeling good. Feeling good and being in a state of empowerment and motivation comes from an internal strength and confidence about where you are going—your vision, passion or a burning desire. And all of this either comes from learning and personal development to strengthen the mind, surrounding yourself with those you want to become or simply by telling yourself enthusiastically that you already are what/who you need to be over and over again until you believe it.

When action comes from inspiration instead of requirement you'll know the feeling of purpose. Inspired action is the kind that will deliver the results you want. When you are driven or compelled to move, when you step forward and do something, you have hit the jackpot. That feeling of compulsion to act has singlehandedly become the driving force of some of the greatest people to have ever lived for they have lived their purpose.

If it weren't for the inspired action of J. K. Rowling, we wouldn't have the legendary Harry Potter children's series that has become an inspiration for many to imagine and dream limitlessly.

If it weren't for the inspired action of Marie Curie, we may not have advanced radiation technology as we know it today, a staple for diagnosis in the medical industry. And if it weren't for the inspired action of Miley Cyrus, we would not know how to twerk. Thank God for Miley. Miley is not exactly the role model I am going for; nonetheless she did teach us something. There are many more great women who took action for something they believed in. They paved the way to show us it is possible for anyone.

TRY THIS ON:

Think about a time in your life when you have felt required to do something, where you have felt obligated to take action. Did this feeling lead to your greatest victory? Did it lead to your best results or your most memorable moment? Probably not. There is a reason why. When you feel required to act, you are moving forward by a feeling of necessity. This often is attached to a negative feeling—a feeling of having to or needing to do something, which in turn will lead to a less than desirable amount of action or quality of action resulting in a less than desirable outcome.

This is not to say we shouldn't do the things that we feel required to do; sometimes these are the key to our greatest victories. However, if the source of your drive comes from inspiration, then the hard stuff is simply necessary and a part of the journey. Think about a time when you were compelled to act. Nothing seemed too big to conquer, and even the limiting beliefs that would normally hold you back seem insignificant or outdated. And, if you're wondering if you have inspired action in your life, you don't. So go find it and you'll find your purpose. Become GREAT.

Inspired action can (and has many times over) lead to movements, change laws, impact nations and, ultimately, change the world. Inspired action is often nothing less than significant in making the world a better place.

At the end of all of this it is your decision to take action. If you don't take action to change your life, then what's ever going to change? You might just need a little help. It's completely normal to feel stuck, but 'normal' isn't what we are going for.

The following is what I have been fortunate enough to learn from some great people in my journey all of which has truly impacted the results I have today. And without each of these messages, this book (along with many other great books) probably wouldn't be in existence.

Find a mentor

We all need guidance from time to time. Usually, it is easier to see if we are screwing up from the outside. I have been so fortunate to have many mentors in my life. They have all played a part in my learning and growth and will continue to do so. Choose wisely, for each will guide you in their way with what they know, which may not be the way you need or want to go.

The first key to finding a mentor is finding someone who has what you want—a job or career, the lifestyle or the achievements. Whatever it is you want find someone who has achieved it already, for they likely know how to then guide someone else achieve it also. Once you have found the person who also aligns with your values and integrity, do exactly as they say. Follow every single word. Listen, watch, and learn. Many people can teach you, but a mentor is someone who leads you to teach yourself.

> "Words do not teach, true knowing comes from life experience."
> —Esther 'Abraham' Hicks

Ask for help

If you need some help (and we all do at times), there is someone out there who has the answer. For a long time I was afraid to ask, the 'lone ranger' living in fear of looking like I didn't already know something I should know. Would people think less of me if I didn't know the answer already? The truth is, in some companies I worked for, yes. As a result I had built a limiting belief out of experiences where I had been reprimanded for asking for help. I learned that asking for help might be a bad thing.

This is BS. Nowhere you work, live, or play should ever make you feel wrong or bad for asking for help. Most of the people who have changed the world have not done so by themselves; they needed an army of support to help them, and they simply weren't afraid to ask for it. It doesn't matter what people think of you; you need to go out there and get what you need to be successful. If you can't change the people around you, then you need to change yourself. Or get some new people around you.

If you don't ask, the answer is always no.

Employ a DIA (Daily Improvement Activity)

Give yourself one task every day, one task that will improve either your mind, your productivity, your results, or relationships. It has been said before that you cannot manage time but you can manage your activity—you just need to set yourself small achievable goals to get started. Small achievable goals are the key to growth and development. They build confidence and belief that you have all the potential in the world, just like everyone else.

So start with something small every day to build the habit of change, either reading ten pages of a book, writing down five things you are grateful for, providing some sort of value to one person, or making a new connection to grow your business. Whatever it is do it religiously every single day. Watch it quickly become a part of your routine and how drastically it can improve your results and how you feel. Ultimately you are doing something for you. Be selfish and prioritize this activity, don't go to bed without having completed it.

"The only thing that changes this world is taking action."
—*Jody Williams*

ENGAGE IN LIFE AND IT WILL ENGAGE IN YOU.

CHAPTER TWENTY-TWO

Belief is the New Black

22

Unicorns and Love Notes

IN SUMMARY OF ALL THE WORK YOU HAVE DONE SO FAR, the limiting beliefs you have unravelled, the empowering beliefs you have ingrained, the big visions you have created for yourself, there are a few more lessons I wish to leave you with. Nine in fact. What I have learned can best be invested helping someone else so consider them love notes from your unicorn. These will be our secret weapons, so keep them stuffed in your bra should you need to ever use them.

FIND THE PARTY THAT'S BEING THROWN FOR YOU AND INVITE YOURSELF.

There is a party being thrown for you out there somewhere. Are you at that party? Or are you at a party for someone else? It's not about the size of the party, it's about the quality of people attending. Some of the best parties I have ever been to included only one other person.

Are you surrounded by supporters? Or are you surrounded by ultimate realists or worse, pessimists who impede on your dreams and insist on telling you why things just don't work out that way?

The power of a group of like-minded people in whatever endeavor can change the world. This was my first step in making any real changes in my life. I had to find people in life who believed in the same things as me, valued the same things as I did, and had the same mission in life. This allowed me to be who and what I wanted to be — a dreamer, a lover, and a girl who wants to change the world. This one change cultivated my ambitions, drove them even higher than I once had thought possible and gave me permission to think big.

Anything else is like a flower trying to grow in cement. This doesn't mean you need to make a huge announcement of your departure from a shit party where you aren't having fun in your straight jacket. Just quietly excuse yourself and head down the hall where the light is brighter and the music suits your taste. Find the party being thrown for you!

UNICORNS ARE EVERYWHERE. NOW PAY ATTENTION!

Years ago I worked for a large technology company in their retail department, which in itself was already ridiculous. Don't get me wrong, I love my iPhone, but I knew nothing other than how to make phone calls and post on Facebook, which was adequate for my daily activities. It wasn't necessary for me to know the inner workings of computers in my role as a leader in the company; however when I stepped onto that sales floor, to a desperate customer needing help- I was a technology-educated employee who should be able to answer their questions. I avoided customers who had tricky questions about hard drives and networks, for the most part, but if I somehow got stuck I'd frantically wave my hand in the air to have a cool uniformed friend beside me in an instant, in case I was asked about microprocessors or RAM.

Once I was asked about batteries by a customer in a hurry with no available uniformed friend in sight. Hmmmm. Do we sell batteries? I've never seen a battery in the store before? Everything plugs into the wall, doesn't it?

At this exact moment as these words leave my mouth in confusion, the world seems to close in on me as the customer reacts with a concerned look on his face (like who let the crazy person out of the padded room?), a friend in unform runs to my defense, saying, "She is new here; batteries are right this way, sir."

Turns out wireless things need batteries. Obviously. And we sold wireless things. It would be almost negligible of the company to not sell batteries; we had a whole shelf devoted to these little things. Not even an hour after the incident, the story had become the talk of the store, with the most prominent joke of the whole situation suggesting that unicorns powered the wireless things, developed by one of the more creative employees at the cash desk. These techie geniuses began working the computers to generate a picture of a unicorn at every computer I stopped to work on, all over the store. I'd be working away and up would flash a unicorn. Surprise! Pay attention!

So unicorns are now my reminder of my goals and what I want, to pay attention because answers and possibility are often right under our nose. They always seem to show up when I need to be listening or noticing something that otherwise I would not. As silly as this sounds, it's actually about awareness. With lives that move so fast, we misunderstand each other all the time. Focus on being aware, and the rest is merely responding accordingly.

DON'T TELL EVERYONE YOU'RE BOOKED IN FOR BOTOX.

If you are driven to grow, there will often be times when you are inspired to take action, improve, or do something big for yourself. These are amazing times—times worth soaking up, celebrating the decision, and enjoying the feelings of motivated change. Whether it is getting Botox or starting a business, don't tell the world no matter how excited or confident in the decision you might be.

The problem is this is hard to do. We are seekers of significance. If we get excited about something, the eyes widen, the chest puffs up, and the parts of the body we use to communicate all get in line to become a samba band announcement. Everyone within a four-foot radius or your most recent text message list is informed or notified and potentially asked for their opinion. What happens next? You get it whether you like it or not. Oftentimes, it's not at all in support. Remember, everyone is employing a different system of beliefs than you, and everyone thinks theirs is right.

Often it's our closest friends and family who are quick to jump and work against your new found decision or inspired action. One of my best friends who was there for me while I grieved over the death of mother for a year, battle depression and anxiety, incoming and outgoing shit boyfriends was the first to pooh-pooh my new business venture and suggest (after a few drinks, mind you) that I was being brainwashed by my new multi-millionaire mentor.

The key word here is **new**. The simple part of all of this is that most people don't like change. It's not the fact that I was changing (your friends won't care less if you get Botox), it was that my friend was impacted by my change. My newfound excitement was affecting her. No longer could we share a few bottles of wine and bitch the night away when I was nothing but positive and full of energy for life.

When those around you fear they might have to change they will likely revolt against your samba band unless they are of a similar mindset or belief. If you aren't completely convinced that similarity exists, then put away the lipstick and get out the glue stick. And if you do spill the beans on the Botox, know that their responses are the best they can come up with based on what they know. Listen to it, but don't heed it unless you can validate with facts that their input is coming from a place of support and/or real experience and results on the matter.

STOP THINKING ABOUT THEM; THEY'VE GOT THAT COVERED.

If you're still talking about that boy who cheated on you in high school, let it go. He certainly isn't hanging onto it. How do I know? He forgot that it even happened. The boy I fell hopelessly in love with in my late teens promised me we would travel the world together, inspired me to take out my three facial piercings and get rid of the bleached blonde hair. He cheated on me with a stripper and blamed me for giving him Chlamydia. After I was given a clean bill of health by the doctor, he insisted he must have contracted it from a toilet seat.

This guy ruined my life for about three weeks until I made the decision to move on. But the emotion of it lasted for a while; I told myself the story of it over and over. I shared it with others like a recount of a World War II battle I took part in with wounds to prove it. It was a sick obsession I had, trying to understand why it happened to me.

When we get hurt by someone we love (or are infatuated with, as I was then), we feel compelled to replay the story in our minds over and over to try and make sense of it. We need to categorize it, assign blame and anger, and make it make sense to eventually move past it.

Years later we reconnected and he nonchalantly suggested we revisit our relationship from years ago. So I brought it up: the cheating, the toilet seat etc (clearly, I hadn't let it go). In shock he responded with concern that I thought all of this and that he didn't really remember why we broke up.

This slap in the face did two things: 1) It made me realize he hadn't put a thought to it in years while I painfully replayed the story over in my mind, and 2) It allowed me to move on.

How many of these stories are you replaying about the same people who have hurt you, broken your heart, or shit on you in some way or other? Do you know these stories by heart, so much that you could line up all your friends and they could spread the good word for you? Here is your wake up call. Stop it. They certainly aren't thinking about you as much as you are about them. So let it go, properly. Every time it comes up in your mind, flip the switch on it and have a ready-to-go story that makes you feel good. I have one. It was something I heard a while back and makes me laugh so much it snaps me out of any story immediately. The second I catch myself in a negative spin or story, I grab for this mantra and repeat it twenty times in my head or aloud. Before long, I'm laughing and I forget what was going through my mind. If you need one until you come up with your own you can borrow mine: "I am a money magnet! You're welcome!"

The truth is most people only care about themselves, which means that's what they are thinking about the majority of the time. It's very much the same way you are thinking about yourself, by focusing on how that person or those people impacted you. So ditch that story and get a new one. And, if you cannot, I suggest you sit down with a pen and paper and some quiet time and focus on:

—**what you can take from the person or experience for which you could be grateful**

—**what you learned from that experience**

—**what you will take with you on the rest of your journey in life**

Thank them for this list, as hard as that may be, then light a little fire and burn the paper if you need to.

SEND 'EM TO THE ISLAND!

My dad is a driving force in my life; he is the person I look up to, emulate, and hope to become in many ways. Apart from the lame jokes and the [9]daggy clothes, he is a kind-hearted, generous, loving person who many people look up to. He often had a little story or suggestion for my seemingly large amount of personality clashes in school. I was mostly a smart ass, but every now and then I would lay down and take an emotional beating from the bigger smart ass and end up at home in tears. Maybe I just liked the drama or the attention. Either way his

9 Australian for 'lame, out of fashion or embarrassing', often used to describe a 'dad'.

suggestions (although completely nonsensical and mostly unorthodox) often worked, much to my surprise.

One particular example I can remember was in grade 5. I had attracted the attention of the class clown, who seemed to find it hilarious to track me down at lunch time and sit on me. This was not only painful (after I struggled for minutes) but also highly embarrassing; it became the joke of the school that the class clown could dominate my small frame to be under his stinky ass within minutes. This all got too much for me one day, after yelling at this kid directly, screaming for help, laughing it off, and telling a teacher to talk to him. I finally had a good cry at home trying to tell my dad what had been happening at school every day.

After a few questions aimed at understanding and probably some patience in finding out his eldest daughter was being sat on by a boy at lunch times in school, he suggested I try something the next time this jerk came toward me. Honestly, I can't believe I listened to his ridiculous suggestion, but what else had I left to do? The next day I went to school and, sure enough, he came right for me at lunch time out in the field. This time, however, I was ready. I had my four best friends lined up with me ready to crouch down on my command. I spotted the kid walking across the field, preparing for the win at hand, and I yelled to my friends… "Three, two, one… go!" We all dropped to our hands and knees and began counting the grass blades one by one. We concentrated hard on it as we knelt down with our face in the patchy fields—no giggling, dead serious, moving through the blades counting one by one.

Out of the corner of my eye I spotted the class clown slowing down in his approach. He seemed confused. As he got closer he almost looked annoyed. "What the hell are you all doing?" he asks exasperated.

"Counting the blades of grass!" I reply in an overly sassy way, with a nervous frog in my throat.

He stood there for a minute with his posse of pimply, scrawny friends, taken aback and a little lost as to what his next move would be (I was already on the ground, so no fun in taking me down).

"This is a stupid idea," he announced and walked away. At long last he was done sitting on me, off to severely annoy another unsuspecting victim, I guess. Who knows and who cares: I was free.

So I began to listen to my dad's suggestions and stories; I had gathered proof that they worked. My dad has always been the leader, the go-to person for others with problems, and he nearly always managed to help solve them. Retired now from over twenty-five years of leading government agencies, he spent a lifetime getting creative to help solve the problems we thought we had.

One trick I will teach my future kids to employ one day has helped me move past much of the shit in my life involving other people. It was a simple idea with big meaning. We as a family had an imaginary island where we would inhabit all the annoying, painful people, the people who got in our way in life. Should one of these people pop up we would announce, "Off to the island!" and banish them forever. Thousands of people collectively have been sent to this island and at this point; I'd hazard a guess that it's overpopulated. We are looking to expand our business to a larger island very shortly.

What an amazing suggestion for a child to use their imagination to ignore those who get in their way. The best part is they are probably all annoying each other over there as we speak. So find an empty island of your own and begin populating it. It'll be the best real estate investment you'll ever make.

FAKE IT 'TIL YOU MAKE IT

As humans, we make stuff up, then we believe it. In fact, this is one of our very special skills. If we just knew how to direct this talent in a positive way, we would be in a very different world today. Most of us make up reasons why we cant be, do and have what we really want..

The statistics are enough to scare most people away. For example… It's been said that approximately 97 percent of the world shares only about 3 percent of the world's money? That means 3 percent of the world's population owns 97 percent of the world's money. The gap is representative of how we think.

Which side of that statistic do you live on? Whichever it happens to be isn't a bad thing, but it is a result of the stories you and

BELIEF IS THE NEW BLACK

the people around you have made up and believed. So if we know what we have is a result of making stuff up and believing it, then why not make up some good stuff and believe it? That's all the 3 percent of the population who owns all the money did. But that sounds a bit like not telling the truth or lying, right? Well, ask yourself how it could be a lie if it hasn't happened yet? It's true if it's in your future, if you chose to believe it.

So let's get some good stories going. Fake it until you've faked it so much you believe it yourself and it's true. When I started my own business and quit my job, my friends called me crazy. They couldn't believe I would leave a secure career with great money and benefits for something unstable that "probably wouldn't work". They were missing the belief I had in myself to make it work.

It's a good thing I had my own story! I had a story and a vision of myself; I was wildly successful and inspiring millions of people. I was living life on my terms. This was far from true at the time. In fact, I had given up everything to go after my dream of owning my own business. I gave up social engagements, a steady income, and shopping (I know!). This was honestly one of the hardest times in my life, but what kept me going was the story of where I was going. I had it so clear in my mind that I believed it, I felt it, and I spoke it. And, low and behold, a few years later, it all came true. Fake it 'til you make it true. Eventually you will.

Your imagination is more powerful than you think. It created the reality around you long before you brought it to life with your actions.

How do we make anything true? Either we find what we consider to be proof or we hear/see it enough. Soon it's as if you saw some proof somewhere along the way but you can't quite remember what it was; you just know it's true now.

We are an easy mark. We convince ourselves of things all the time, which is an amazing quality once you can teach yourself how to use it to change the way you think. If not it's still an amazing quality and probably the reason you don't have what you want.

Put the story on repeat until you believe it. You believed in the tooth fairy once, didn't you? Santa Claus? Your parents sold you on something you wanted to be true, like magic. You still have this ability to believe. Find the reason you need to believe in magic again and you will. Act as if and make it real. It's only fake if you believe it so.

"The most common way people give up their power is by thinking they don't have any."
—Alice Walker

BE YOUR OWN HERO

I grew up idolizing many great women, but one stood out: Marilyn Monroe. I have no idea where it came from, but something in me just loved everything about her. I studied her movies, read about her life, and looked at pictures of her for hours on end. Something about her spirit attracted me to her as an icon, a leader, and someone I wanted to emulate. I became obsessed with connecting to this power in some way or other. Deep down I know it was a comparison; I wanted to be her. She exuded so much beauty and admiration, she garnered so much attention, and she had accomplished so much in such a short, courageous life.

We all have these women we look up to, our heroes. For whatever reason we look to others for the greatness, beauty, strength, and power we want in ourselves. We somehow think all of this is found outside of ourselves. The beautiful part about this is that it's all readily available, inside of you. What I was looking for in Marilyn was inside of me; it was just covered up under some very limiting beliefs and excuses as to why I didn't have the courage to become who I thought she was and ultimately who I wanted to be. So one day I thought about all the things I loved about her: her beauty, grace, confidence, connection to people, and the energy and fun-loving attitude she possessed. Then I put it on paper. It was a giant list of all the things I wanted to be, the greatness I saw within her that had attracted me to her.

I looked at this list every day and visualized myself as Marilyn. I even dressed up as her a few times. But, by looking at the qualities I admired, as if they were separate from her and available to anyone, I realized I could become them. They weren't tied to her and only her. So I began to embody them myself; I could feel great, feel beauty, feel strength. These feelings are, after all, a choice and something we are all capable of.

What I loved and admired about Marilyn wasn't necessarily her physical beauty, but it was her power, strength, and courage—the qualities we often look for in a hero.

Marilyn Monroe illuminated others by being illuminated. If you want to light up the world, you must first light up yourself and the world will follow.

So, who's your hero? Write down what you admire and love about this person, then read it to yourself every day. Become your own hero, become the greatness that you see in others. It may take some practice, but it's the fun part of life. Play dress up, put your big beautiful cape on (imagined or real), and BE your own hero. You never know, you may become someone else's hero in the process!

GET SOME DIRT UNDER YOUR NAILS

Okay, ladies, now I love a manicure as much as the next diva, but ain't no manicure ever saved the world or yourself. Do yourself a favor and get your hands dirty. This means do some dirty work, make a mess! You've probably heard before that life is not a dress rehearsal; we can't rewind, so this is it. Get in the game or watch from the sidelines because others will take the opportunities you don't.

Somewhere along the way we have become confused about what it means to be driven and motivated toward a goal. We think just to have them is enough and somehow it will show up. The only people who get things done are the ones who are out there doing it. You can choose to be passive and watch life ride on by or you can do what needs to be done to get what you want. Once you start, you won't ever want to stop.

Take this book for example. I have had many people in the process of writing this say to me, "I have always wanted to write a book," or "I wish I could write a book." So I ask them, "Well, why don't you? What follows is nothing short of a slew of reasons why they can't or don't know how. I didn't know how but I figured it out. That is always the way: if you want something badly enough, you will figure it out.

"I'm tough, ambitious, and I know exactly what I want. If that makes me a bitch, okay."
—Madonna

Speaking of bitches... I said dirt, not blood. So let's keep it clean, ladies. Do not pull the hair of the bitch you'll need help from later.

'I NEVER GOT A HOLE IN MY PANTYHOSE,' SAID NO WOMAN EVER

Another way to say this is, "I have never failed," said no successful person ever. In fact, failing is the only way to succeed. How else would you know how to improve? If you are only succeeding, you probably aren't taking enough risks. The biggest failures often lead to the biggest success. The trick is not to focus all your energy on the failing. Get what you needed to learn and move on quickly.

When I first stepped out as an entrepreneur and started my own business it took off. In a big way it exploded and I couldn't keep up. Slowly however, I lost the momentum; I couldn't manage the demands, and I was drowning quickly with no way of knowing how to get out alive. So I lost the business and ended up back at square one. I spent a little bit of time feeling sorry for myself, wishing it could have been different, but it was only the decision to get back up and try again that changed anything. Sure, I lost money and some time, but I gained valuable experience in the process. That experience has helped me bring more money and time to my life —a direct result of having failed in the first place.

Not only did I head back in for another round—stronger, wiser, and better equipped—I now knew what big failure felt like.

Was it the worst thing that ever happened? No. Not even close. Now the inevitable failure ahead is manageable and actually motivating. I know I can withstand greater challenges and come out on top, and that is an empowering place to be.

The point of failure is not just to learn but to know you can fail and still survive. Courage is built out of every survived failure.

JUST LOVE.

One of the most amazing women I have ever known is someone I have never actually met in person. What started out as a brief business introduction over Skype has led to one of the most profound friendships I will cherish for the rest of my life. Loretta (Lou) Honeychurch, whom you will hear from at the conclusion of this book, played a big part in the evolution of it- much bigger than I think even she realizes.

I have always heard that if you come from a place of love, everything and everyone can be forgiven, understood, and accepted. I just never knew how. How do you come from a place of love? We are so programmed to think the negative first, to jump to conclusions and assume the worst. So how do we put all of the kneejerk emotional reactions aside and consciously make a decision to love?

This is what my beautiful friend taught me by example and instruction. It's something I will forever be learning in life and may never master. But, by choosing to try, I know I have already made a difference within myself. To just love is one of the hardest things to do, especially in the face of pain. Yet it's probably the only thing that can truly set you free.

How do you get better at something? You practice. Lou taught me to practice. Practice choosing love.

TRY THIS ON:

Think of someone in your life who is causing you to feel stress or hurt or anger right now. Notice how you can feel it? You can bring up the emotion at any time; this is how powerful you are.

So now close your eyes and imagine you are inside your heart. Picture yourself radiating heat from your heart. You are in it, feeling love, focused on love, inside the beautiful bubble of your heart. Feel it? Warm and fuzzies!

Now picture that person again but stay in your heart, stay in that beautiful place of love and picture that person. Notice how much harder it is to feel the same level of stress, hurt or anger toward them when coming from this place of love? And all you did was change your state, your vibration, your emotion. You chose to feel love first and as a result the yucky feeling was harder to find, harder to feel.

What a beautiful thing to practice, to choose love. Now practice this! Practice coming from this place as often as possible; close your eyes and really feel it. Know that it's a choice and one you can choose any time to change your state. This one activity will change your entire life, if you let it. Love makes the world go 'round, and so can you.

"It is our choices that show what we truly are, far more than our abilities."
—J. K. Rowling

CHAPTER TWENTY-THREE
Belief is the New Black

23
Understand Belief, Change Your World

Take out the piece of paper from the back of the book that you tucked away for later. Later is now. Have a look at it. Knowing what you now know, having the the experiences you've had while reading this book and reflecting on your own life- do you still feel strongly about what you wrote? Are your observations on the paper the same observations you would make now? What's changed? Do you feel different? Possibly distant from the ideas written on that piece of paper however long ago that may have been? Notice the change, however small or drastic it may be, it's a new awareness.

Congratulations! What else is now possible?

When you can truly start to grow in your choices and decisions you'll see the miraculous evidence show up as a result of your change. You will realize just how powerful you are. Our beliefs are at the core of any change within us, and learning how to choose the right ones begins with listening to yourself and paying attention to how you feel.

What's working for you? And what's not? It can be that simple, but we dramatize and complicate to no end and with little happiness. My aim in all of these stories and observations is to poke a hole in those otherwise bulletproof beliefs we all have. My goal is to show you some proof that you can have what you want. But it starts with you. And only you. You just might need a little push off the ledge and maybe some guidance, as did I.

After my mum left this world, I was looking for the answer—looking for someone to show me the way or help me understand. I was looking outside of myself as we often do when we think we don't have the answers; otherwise, why would we feel this way if we had a different option available to us?

What I've realized in my journey is that the journey itself is in fact to figure it out, to know yourself, to learn for yourself how to choose, create, and become what you want. And no two journeys are the same—yours will be different from mine. But we can learn from each other along the way.

One defining moment for me was a conversation by the ocean at a small seaside café on the southern end of San Diego—one of the most beautiful small cities I have seen. The conversation itself was nothing really spiritual or overly enlightening, and I wasn't actually focused on the words being exchanged. I just knew I was in the company of love. I had momentarily left the conversation to gaze out at the ocean, and for whatever reason I was deep in thought about my mum. I was thinking about time and experiences, which were lost forever. I could feel the usual sadness coming over me and for some reason I had chosen this moment to really connect with the emotion of what had happened to me and my life as a result of her death.

This time was different. It was more than the typical pain I would feel when I thought of her, the loss and the sadness. This time my mind started to wander off in a different direction. A direction of hope. I began to think forward instead of backward, and forward wasn't sad. Forward wasn't the pain I knew so well. It was different, brighter, and more alive. It was a sense of happiness as I started to think about what I could do. Suddenly (after a year of so much emotional pain and guilt), I felt happy. I could feel happiness as I chose a forward direction. A rush of emotion flushed to my face and tears welled in my eyes as realized I had found a better story. It was one that felt better. Whatever I had been waiting for to heal me hadn't come, so I had somehow decided in that moment to go to it. I chose love.

And as if someone spoke to me in my mind, out loud I heard, "Be the change."

Now I realize this is the popularized adaptation to a famous Gandhi quote, "If we could change ourselves, the tendencies in the world would also change. As a man changes his own nature, so does the attitude of the world change toward him. We need not wait to see what others do."

So either Gandhi was speaking to me telepathically or my unconscious mind pulled out the file I needed and shoved it in my face. Either origin is fine by me but the point was I felt it. Be the change you wish to see in the world. Be who you need to be to be to choose love. It's not like I had any more discussion around how to do this prior to this breakthrough, but somehow I knew I could. I had made the decision in that moment to surge forward in life and be the change, be what I was waiting for, be what I was looking for in other people, be what I wanted my mum to be. In all of this I began to feel a sense of calm like I hadn't felt in years, a sense of serenity and a sense of peacefulness. I felt love.

With a renewed energy I found my purpose and went to work on what you have just read. This is one small part of my decision to be the change but one small part that took a massive leap across boundaries I didn't even know I had when I started. And, through this beautiful reflection, I have come to truly understand how powerful we are — each of us, both individually and collectively. When we can accept our gifts, and learn to give them, this becomes our legacy. Mine is a legacy of love. This is one of my empowering beliefs.

"The day the power of love overrules the love of power, the world will know peace."
—Mahatma Gandhi

…and so will you.

Belief is the new Black.

Love,
MARNIE KAY

CLOSING LETTER...

Belief is the New Black

Dear Mum,

I cry as I finish this book not with tears of sadness anymore but with tears of joy as I embark on a journey with a message.

What I have learned in my life through my experiences is valuable to the world and I choose to give it on behalf of us, you and me.

I cherish both the beautiful memories we have today and the ones I will imagine as we travel the world together for the rest of my existence on this planet, and beyond. The love you so longed for was there all along, as is mine—inside of us. We live it now together as one. Our gift to the world.

I love you.

MARNIE

Belief is everything, everything is belief.

Afterword

BY LORETTA (LOU) HONEYCHURCH

IT'S TIME TO WAKE UP. It's time to move forward and live the life of your dreams. It's time to be who you truly are, to express your true essence and bring forth the joy and love that is you.

Easier said than done, right? Not really. What if I told you all you had to do was believe that anything was possible? What if I told you that you have the ability to live the most extraordinary life imaginable? How would you respond? Would you believe me?

Belief is a big thing; it's the key to living your best possible life. Yet it seems to be the one thing that we keep missing. Why is that? Because to believe in ourselves means playing outside the safety zone. And that's a scary place. Fear plays a big part in stopping us from being who we really are. When fear enters our life we almost become unrecognizable. We should be more afraid of staying in the safety zone. That's a place where life goes unexpressed, unexplored, and unfulfilled.

WHAT DO YOU BELIEVE?

If you are someone who believes that dreams are for other people, ask yourself, at what point in my life did I choose to separate myself from my true potential? How often have you felt like you were living on the outside of life looking in, watching other people fulfill their dreams, wondering why they can and you can't. I've had that feeling. I gave up on my dreams when I was twelve. I don't remember why. I was in my thirties before I realized that way back then I had made a decision based on a belief that wasn't true. You may have done the same thing, just as Marnie did. But we also have a choice… to believe that we can make our dreams come true and that anything is possible. Now I get to participate in the creation of my amazing life.

We all have a story. Our stories consist of the material of our lives, good and bad. It's how we choose to allow our stories to define us that makes the difference. Through her beautiful story, Marnie reveals the pain that ultimately led her to discover a strength and courage beyond words. When she brought belief back into her life she emerged as a passionate and inspiring woman with limitless options, on a mission to help others.

When I first read Marnie's manuscript I realized that we all share a similar journey. Our stories are not the same but the deep, unwavering feeling that there is more to us than "this" is something that every one of us feels at some time. Because there is more to us, and even when you think you have it all, you will desire more. Because you are capable of more. You have the infinite capacity to be more and create more. Desire is hardwired into our programming.

I am deeply moved by Marnie's courage in writing this book. I know she had to confront some emotions that were painful. It was so worth it. Her story reminds us that to be extraordinary doesn't require any special talent. It's all already there in the blueprint that is you — waiting to be brought into reality.

What you now hold in your hands is a manual for tapping into your potential. *Belief Is the New Black* will challenge you to think differently about who you are and what is possible in your life. Marnie and I share a similar experience of coming into our own unique power so I can personally vouch for everything she teaches. Human beings are miracles of life. We are exquisite in nature and form with capabilities far beyond that which we are aware of.

I have been fortunate in life to be surrounded by amazing people who are living examples of what is possible. Marnie is certainly one of them: a divine spirit who shines so brightly it's blinding. I am so proud of her and I feel blessed to have her my life.

I am speaking for Marnie when I say that, through writing this book and exploring the difficult moments in her life, she has also discovered the true depth of her ability as a woman, a spirit, and as an incredible human being. That is the gift. Her book is perfect.

—LORETTA (LOU) HONEYCHURCH
www.lorettahoneychurch.com | loretta@lorettahoneychurch.com

A LETTER FOR THE WORLD
ON COURAGE. FROM MY
BEAUTIFUL AND POWERFUL
SOULFRIENDS...
ASHLEY AND JENNIFER
GOULART

Belief is the New Black

Our Story

IT WAS A HOT SUMMER DAY BACK IN 1986—wait, scratch that! We all know the story of how we got here; the question is what did we do after that? Who did we become?

When we were asked by Marnie to be a part of her book, it was a shocker for us. Us? Really? And then we stepped back and took a look at what this book represented: transformation, belief, and love. Beautiful women at their finest, we realized that we represented all of these. As women, it is difficult for us to look at ourselves in that way. And why shouldn't we? We all have beautiful and unique gifts and stories and sharing those stories of ourselves is the biggest vulnerability of all. But you can't seek change, love, and transformation without the sacrifice of vulnerability. So here we are being vulnerable... to Marnie, to ourselves, and to everyone single, beautiful woman who walks the Earth.

Our transformation began as children. In fact, we have been in transition our whole lives. It's something you don't understand and realize at first, of course, but vital to every aspect of our lives.

Our childhood wasn't the picture perfect upbringing. We came from a broken home (our parents separated in 1997) and that is when our transformation really started. Our home life became a single parent style. Our beautiful mother was doing all she could to keep afloat.

A year after our parents separated our mother became very ill with depression. When your life source crumbles, you can't help but feel like you are crumbling, too. I (Jennifer) suffered from the eating disorder, bulimia. Everything around me was losing grip. The girls at school bullied me every single day. They called me ugly, stupid, and would gather the biggest rocks they could find and threw them at me. It went as far as them following me to the bathroom and attacking me inside of the stalls. They wanted me to die, and sometimes I felt like I wanted to, too.

I hated who I was. I was ashamed. The eating disorder wasn't about me wanting to be skinny. I wanted to get rid of all the bad stuff about me. I hated the way I looked, I was deathly skinny and I wore oversized clothing so no one would notice. But one day my mother (and my sister's behind her) literally knocked the door down of the washroom, barged in grabbed me and with tears in her eyes my mother screamed, "Stop it!" We all sat together and cried. That was the day

I stood up to my eating disorder, and that night was the last time those girls ever bullied me.

My sisters and I formed an alliance and we took a stand. Our mother was still in a dark place, but we stood up for her, and for one another. It was hard sometimes. We were angry at some points. So much was happening in our lives. But we knew even then that strength knew no age or boundary. Our mother did everything she could to protect us, and here our turn was to do the same. We became her glue (along with our older sister, Melissa.) We formed an ally of strength, love, and courage, and because of that our mother became strong again and so did Jen. She was lost, and because of our undying love for her, we became her light. Love is such a powerful thing. Love is what we owe a majority of our life to!

Life moved on for us. We graduated high school, our big sister got married, and we started to lead our own lives. Life was good.

In 2008, life struck us hard once again, this time it was me (Ashley). I was diagnosed with severe OCD and depression put on medication to numb me out. That is exactly what I felt like. This rollercoaster became even bigger than the one before. I became lost in a profound darkness. Nothing anyone said or did could save me. In fact it made me angry when everyone did, and it made me angry when no one tried. I quit my job, locked myself inside for months, and wasted away. Literally, the life drained from my eyes, my heart, and my body.

I was fragile. My clothes hung off my body like a coat rack, and my lifeline was running thin. I didn't eat, didn't sleep, and didn't move. I sat in silence, lost in my thoughts, pain, and misery. It was my only friend at the time. I didn't want to be on earth anymore, and every single day I contemplated taking my own life.

It was hard for me (Jennifer) to watch my best friend suffer so significantly, and not being able to reach out, understand, or even help her. She refused everything. She rejected any love I tried to give. She was dying inside and it was killing us all to watch.

2010 was the breaking point. I (Ashley) began to really think of ending my life. I sat in the washroom with scissors in hand ready to end all the pain and suffering. It was there, right at my wrist and for some reason I looked up and saw my reflection in the mirror. My hair was wild, my face red and wet from the tears and pain, and I screamed with every ounce of my being, "Enough!" The scream was so strong and powerful that I shook and collapsed to the floor. I rolled into a ball and shook uncontrollably for thirty minutes straight. I was paralyzed.

I got up, picked up the phone and called Jen at work. When I (Jennifer) answered her call, all I could hear was Ashley crying, barely being able to make out what she was saying. "Jen, I am not okay," she said. "I keep wanting to die, and I don't want to die, Jen, I want to live." I responded, "If you die Ash, I die too. And I am not ready to die, and I won't let you."

That same night Ashley enrolled herself into therapy and started taking the first steps into transformation and medication free!

Many people think there are no second chances in life, and we beg to differ. We get one life, the one we live right now in the present. And the funny thing is, life is all about chances and choices. Waking up every day is a chance to make a choice to change your life, whatever the circumstance. We got hit with hard ones; many people do, and we decided to take a chance and make a change to better ourselves.

Being a woman is beautiful. Being a powerful woman, with conviction, discernment, determination, and love is an immeasurable force. It doesn't matter if you are twelve, seventeen, or forty, the power of change doesn't have a timeline or age cap. All it requires is profound courage. We declared to ourselves, to our families, and to the world that we would be powerful women. We would learn to love ourselves wholeheartedly, both internally and externally. We would show our strength and compassion toward every single person we met. We could be ashamed of our lives and what it gave to us, the hands that were dealt, or we could live in eternal gratitude. We could be proud that we stood up and tall, regardless of the undefeatable circumstances that looked like they would never end. There is no light at the end of the tunnel, the light is within. We only understood our paths, once we recognized our fire. Fire is passion, it's the fuel to the light within. You can't have life without fire.

So, here we are now, owners of our own company (The Superior Man), living as writers and teachers. We used the ground of rock bottom as our foundation, and we used the stones thrown at us as the stairway to love. Life is an extraordinary gift and learning to be a womanly warrior is the greatest achievement we have done to date. We decided to be powerfully beautiful in darkness and shade, because we are forces to be reckoned with!

Our advice to all women is understand that courage is madness and beauty. Courage is your change, your love, and your light! Don't ever stop shining! Don't ever stop being courageous! The best things in life are the things we have the courage to feel, do, and change!

Thank you, Marnie Kay, for being a lighthouse of dreams for women across the world. It is both an honor and a gift to share in this with you and be in your presence. For your womanly power, we are eternally grateful!

BE A WOMAN WARRIOR LADIES!

—Ashley & Jennifer Goulart

About the Author

MARNIE K·AY

AUSSIE AT HEART, CANADIAN AT HAND, Marnie Kay once said she would follow the summer months around the world. Today that is the life she enjoys while she writes, teaches and inspires thousands of women all over the world, on a mission to share the idea of a world where women empower women through education and stories of strength, courage, inspiration and belief.

This wasn't the life she was living just a few short years ago. With a high-powered corporate career leading thousands of people and millions of dollars in business in North America by the age of 27, Marnie was lost. With years of diagnosed depression, anxiety, an estranged relationship with her mother and on the constant verge of what's commonly known as 'burnout' Marnie was looking for the answer. It was at this time, when Marnie needed her most, that her mother died suddenly of heart disease. This changed everything.

Searching for answers, Marnie became fascinated with the idea of belief. After a traumatic event full of grief, anger and sadness, she realized everything that had once made sense to her was shattered. What was once important no longer was, what was once the 'truth' about herself was now a lie. Marnie discovered everything she believed was simply a story she was telling herself.

What a powerful concept.

This book, 'Belief is the new Black' details her experience, the revelation or 'AHA moment' and her study into the power of belief- what it is, how it works and what to do about it.

Everything we think, do and say is powered by our inner beliefs- most of which just aren't true. My mission is to inspire women all over the world with the idea that they needn't wait for a traumatic experience to change their lives. If they want to change their lives for the better, they just need to know they can and take a small step forward. The belief will come. Often we search for our greatness in those around us, yet our true greatness can only come from within. And it's in there I promise!

Love,

MARNIE KAY

Visit the author online at

WWW.MARNIEKAY.COM
WWW.BELIEFISTHENEWBLACK.COM
E: info@MARNIEKAY.COM

&

#BeliefIsTheNewBlack

Family
PHOTOS

Mum in her mum's
arms, 1960

Dad 'Look I made a
baby' 1984

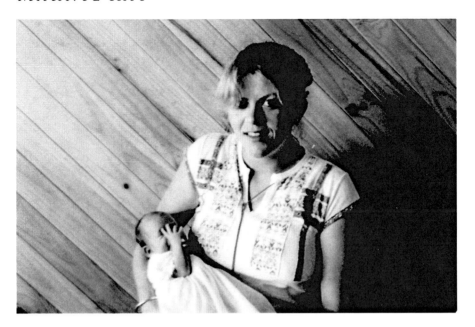

Me in Mum's arms, 1984

Me, after a good cry, 1988ish

3 kids later, Rob, Mum, Carly, Me, 1994ish

Mum, my sister Carly's wedding, me & Rob, 2008

My dad. My prom, his hair, 2001

The only photo I said I'd use.

Dad, My hero & I in New York, 2014

Wendy Kay 1960– 2011
Virgo, lover of travel, sweet
stuff & love.

Be A Female Millionaire

with
Amy Beilharz

HELPING YOU MOVE FROM SURVIVING TO THRIVING!

Amy helps women create more meaning,
have more influence, and experience more freedom!

To learn more visit

www.BeAFemaleMillionaire.com

LOVE+*lifestyle*
MEDIA GROUP

AVANT GARDE INTELLECTUAL INSPIRATION
...where luxury and intellectualism find cohesion.

www.lovelifestylemedia.com

LOVE + Lifestyle Media Group is a virtual publishing house that makes the book creation process effortless for authors that want to create a lasting impression.

Our self-publishing custom design firm offers books in paperback, hardcover and digital formats with worldwide distribution.

| Editorial | Design | Print | Marketing | PR | Distribution |

info@lovelifestylemedia.com

CHOFESH
BOOKS

Chofesh (means freedom or to be free) Books inspires women to live free. We want you to share your life journey to help promote emotional freedom.

The books we publish under Chofesh will be bring women to a higher level of consciousness surrounding their mind, health and wealth. We want to innovate self-development concepts from being conveyed in the traditional format creating a more real, honest dialogue for our readers. Life innovation and inspiration should be exciting and the message that our authors want to convey in their books should be reflective of that freedom visually.

BELIEF IS THE NEW BLACK

CPSIA information can be obtained at www.ICGtesting.com
Printed in the USA
LVOW10s0551120315

430189LV00014B/70/P